# The Application of

# Impossible Things

## My Near Death
## Experience in Iraq

### By Natalie Sudman

OZARK
MOUNTAIN
PUBLISHING

PO Box 754, Huntsville, AR 72740
800-935-0045 or 479-738-2348; fax 479-738-2448
www.ozarkmt.com

For permission, serialization, condensation, adaptions, or for our catalog of other publications, write to Ozark Mountain Publishing, Inc., P.O. box 754, Huntsville, AR 72740, ATTN: Permissions Department.

**Library of Congress Cataloging-in-Publication Data**

Sudman, Natalie, 1960-
  *Application of Impossible Things - My Near Death Experience in Iraq*,
by Natalie Sudman
Natalie's near death experience when her truck was hit with a roadside bomb in Iraq. She recalls the entire spirit side experience as they repair her body so she could live.
1. Near Death Experience 2. Iraq 3. Spirit Side 4. Metaphysics
I. Sudman, Natalie, 1960-  II. Metaphysics  III. Iraq  IV. Title

Library of Congress Catalog Card Number: 2011945965

ISBN: 978-1-886940-24-6


Cover Art and Layout: Victoria Cooper Art
Book set in: Times New Roman
Book Design: Julia Degan

Published by:

OZARK
MOUNTAIN
PUBLISHING
PO Box 754
Huntsville, AR 72740

WWW.OZARKMT.COM
Printed in the United States of America

# Table of Contents

Author's Note                                                    i
Preface                                                          ii

Chapter 1   The Catalyst                                         1
Chapter 2   The Environment                                      9
Chapter 3   Personalities, Interaction, and Intent              21
Chapter 4   Choice, Purpose, and Responsibility                 33
Chapter 5   Skills and the Consciousness/Body Connection        47
Chapter 6   R and R                                             57
Chapter 7   Healing and Assistance                              69
Chapter 8   Jumping Off                                          81
Chapter 9   The Application of Impossible Things                 89

Glossary                                                        119

# Author's Note

Getting blown up was not a solo event, but the experiences and interpretations set forth in this book are mine alone. To my knowledge, no one else present during the incident recalls any similar experiences. My guess is that if any of them become aware of this book, they will shake their heads, roll their eyes, and attribute my memories to hallucinations of stress or the unfortunate side effects of severe concussion. Some will be embarrassed on my behalf, bless their generous hearts.

In an effort to protect the privacy of others who were present during and after the incident, names of individuals have been changed, place names have been avoided, and dates have been deliberately omitted.

If any of those people do happen read this book, though, I want to thank you from the bottom of my soul. Thank you for carrying me to safety and patching me up while I blabbered on morphine. Thank you for operating on me with such fine results, and for flying me from place to place in your helos* and C130s. Thank you for worrying about me, caring for me with attention and humor, and for pushing me when I needed it. Thank you for listening and patiently answering my endless questions, and thank you for laughing with me—and at me! Thank you for dealing with the horrors of federal paperwork involved when an army civilian is blown up and for insisting on a place for my care within the military facilities, then monitoring the quality of that care. Thank you for calling me on the phone from far-flung places and for visiting me and telling me I looked good when I looked like shit. Thank you for bringing me amazing gifts ... all those anonymous strangers just walking into my room: who were all of you angels?! Thank you for sending emails and funny cards and colorful flowers and seeds that grew as my body healed. Thank you for presenting me with medals that I didn't deserve and for believing that I did deserve them. Thank you for including me in your prayers and thoughts though I'd never even met most of you. I was, and still am, overwhelmed and profoundly moved by having been on the receiving end of such an unimaginable outpouring of care and generosity.

I will always look for ways to pass that beauty forward.

# PREFACE

I was blown up in a roadside bomb attack in Iraq. The incident has had lasting effects on my physical life: vision in my right eye was affected, and I still have limited mobility in one wrist and shoulder. Small titanium patches cover holes in my skull.

Within the context of working in Iraq, getting blown up is an interesting (if rather histrionic) memory that gains its full value when viewed through the complex whole of the war environment and the work that I did there. Those memories describe a trajectory and an environment that would fill a book—but not this book.

Rather than focusing on a broad perspective by relating a story of sixteen months working in Iraq administering construction contracts for the US Army, in this book I intend to stay narrow, digging into what took place within a few short seconds at the time of the explosion. Or perhaps between seconds. When our truck was hit by the improvised explosive device (IED), I had what the paranormal community would refer to as an out-of-body experience.

I use the out-of-body or OBE designation without being certain it's the best description. Near death experience or NDE, might also be accurate. When the explosion occurred, I immediately left my body. I didn't experience the classic tunnel of light that others have reported. I simply blinked to another place, one that was familiar in essence. I was conscious, and I know—not *believe*—that what I experienced was real.

I'd like to think that telling this story and exploring some of its details and implications might in some way assist others, yet I approach it with some internal resistance. My reasons for hesitation have to do with issues that many others must recognize: fear and insecurity. First and foremost, I hesitate to expose a low-profile paranormal awareness to the general public and thus open myself to the possibility of ridicule and scorn of particular and various friends whose connections I value. Responding to skepticism by listening politely can be tedious. Engaging skeptics in dialogue about psychic phenomena is rarely fruitful.

Secondly, I question whether I own appropriate authority to write about things that others may be able to address more clearly or with greater depth and assurance. This is not to say that I don't trust my own perception or my personal authority but rather an acknowledgement that people prefer a solid string of proven past performance in a writer. If I could cite a few scientific studies of psi phenomena in which I'd participated and produced amazing results or if I introduced myself by providing proof of a few years' worth of amazing psychic predictions, perhaps I'd be more comfortable introducing myself. I present none of those credentials.

Finally, similar experiences have been recounted in many books. Why add another?

Some recent events have forced me to admit to myself that certain things that come easily and naturally to me are not necessarily easy and instinctive for others. What people seek through a burgeoning choice of institutes, classes, groups and belief systems, I have to admit I've always known and frequently put to use. At times I've buried the skills or tried to deny them, but being of my *essence*, they're impossible to actually lose. And finding life unbearably dull or alarmingly sloppy without their use keeps prompting me to return to them.

Since I was a child, I've had precognitive dreams and waking "visions." Ever since I can remember, I've been acutely aware of the energy of buildings and old battlefields and have often seen and interacted with spirits. I've had out-of-body experiences, given accurate psychic readings for friends and strangers, and journeyed through worlds and dimensions as shamans do. As evidence, however, I can't comfortably present these experiences as proof or validation of any authority I might have in the subject of the paranormal. In only a few instances have I shared an experience with someone who could attest to its truth.

My internal assurance of the validity of what I know to be true, then, is currently my only authority for addressing subjects that fall under the broad category of the paranormal. The final impetus to set aside my fears and insecurities in order to write this story is the possibility that there may be people like me out there who have had similar experiences and want to know that they aren't the only ones fumbling around on their own. Or that there may be people who want to know more yet haven't found the particular voice that they connect with, the voice that causes them to think, *Yes! Yes! Me, too!* Most of the voices that I've found in books and media are, frankly, not ones that I connect with for various reasons that first express themselves most easily in negatives: I don't believe that I have to join an ashram, study with the Dalai Lama, sweat with an Amerindian, drink ayahuasca with a Peruvian shaman, pay thousands of dollars for a workshop, or otherwise participate in someone's belief system to reach wisdom, touch nirvana, perform miracles, connect with my higher self or a creator, or achieve oneness with all. I don't believe that there are universal dream symbologies or universally applicable interpretations for the appearance of animals in one's life. I don't believe that I require crystals, scents, or food regimes to raise my vibrational awareness or capacity. I don't believe that someone else holds the key to my path to enlightenment. I don't believe that others' rituals will necessarily work well for me, or that what I see is more valid than what they see, or that I can create absolutely anything that I want in life by following their ten steps. I don't believe my experiences or skills make me more valuable or special than other people. My experiences and explorations suggest that the tools, props, and disciplines espoused by spiritual groups and individual interests are ultimately unnecessary. They can be invaluable *starting* points or training tools, but they are not *requirements* and can at worst become impediments to personal exploration, expansion, and finding answers to one's own best questions.

Expressed in the positive, I believe that the paranormal is normal. I believe that we all have the natural capacity of various psychic sensitivities though some people may have more natural skill or talent in the same way some have a more natural talent for music or baseball. I know the limiting power of fears and cultural programming that we carry without really being aware of the influence they have on our lives. I believe science is capable of describing some energies known to paranormal practitioners and would already have done so if only the bulk of the scientific world would quit insisting that something doesn't exist just because it hasn't been described or doesn't fit current theory (which is, after all, *theory*). I believe that the tools offered through books, training programs, individual teachers and gurus (including scientists and clergy), are valuable only up to the point that they're left behind, and students become their own teachers. I believe that we each choose to experience our lives *as they are* while continuing to learn, create, and change from that present moment, always, in some way, enhancing us as whole beings, as well as enhancing each other's experiences here in the physical universe—most often unconsciously but always with each other's consent. And I believe in the profound value of taking personal responsibility for everything that I create and experience in my life.

I also believe in my own ineptitude and confusion within that creation and experience while simultaneously being perfectly and profoundly whole and at peace.

Although similar experiences of OBEs or NDEs have drastically changed others' understandings of reality, my experience has acted as a confirmation and expansion. I've experienced paranormal phenomena ever since I can remember, and though I did learn to keep most of those perceptions to myself, I generally retain a trust in my experiences regardless of the cultural programming that incessantly claims it to be fiction. So although I won't describe my OBE experience as a revolution, it is part of an ongoing personal evolution, and, in conjunction with the physical effects of having been blown up, it has affected my life.

Setting aside my fears and insecurities, then, I've decided to write about my experiences and thoughts regarding it, both for my own enjoyment and in hopes of continuing expansion through dialogue. And if what I've experienced proves valuable to even one person who reads this book, I'll consider that to have been far more useful than protecting my petty fears.

Note: A glossary can be found at the back of the book for those readers unfamiliar with military slang. Words found in the glossary are marked with an asterisk in the text.

# Chapter 1
# The Catalyst

I had just closed my eyes, hand propping up my head, elbow on the door handle. It was the end of a long day of construction site visits and now only a few minutes out from base. I'd long ago quit paying attention to what was passing by outside the window and had lost track of how far we were from the rest of our security convoy. This team seemed to travel with a half kilometer or more of road between wagons, and I hadn't seen the Iraqi police escort for a while. Not knowing the two security men in the front seats well, I hadn't chatted with them. Some men prefer to rivet their attention on the environment; they weren't talking with each other, so I felt they might not welcome questions or comments from me. The team was running on closed mic*, a stupifyingly dull way to travel in the back seat of an armored Land Cruiser, cut out of the chatter of hyper-aware security men informed by multiple sets of alert senses. As a passenger, I'd hit the familiar point of being artificially lulled into boredom.

All I heard was a "pop"—the sound of a champagne cork from one hundred meters—the Microsoft sound of opening a new window—a finger snap from across the office.

I vividly remember taking a long, deep breath—more of a sigh that echoed an internal sigh. I thought, Shit. I was tired inside, exhausted from long days spent

1

**trying to train a new project manager while catching up with a demanding workload after an insufficient two weeks of leave. I didn't want something hard, something that would require effort. I wanted to rest.**

**Tough luck.**

**Get on with it, I told myself.**

**I opened my eyes.**

This is a portion of an account of the incident written shortly after I was discharged from Walter Reed Army Medical Center. I'd relived the story over and over in my mind during my month as an inpatient, deliberately and ruthlessly attempting to maintain only that which I truly remembered. Adding and subtracting from memory is easy—we all do it, and do it casually. Determined to avoid that fiction, as I thought of it, I hoped to use the incident in a book about my sixteen months administering reconstruction contracts in Iraq. I wanted the entire account to be as accurate to my own memory as possible, without resorting to histrionic descriptions of war. I was determined not to get sucked into the politics of a simplistic ideological support or condemnation of our efforts in Iraq, or get mired in creating an enthusiastic glorification or indignant diatribe on corruption and disgrace within the reconstruction effort. *Bang-bang* sells in any form, but I believe more complex stories contain valuable truths. I wanted to be able to relate the experience in a way that faithfully described the fine and wonderfully wild condensation of humanity with its rich complexities and paradoxes, ending up somewhere that mattered.

So the details recounted above are all true—unless omission counts as a lie. For all my insistence on telling things straight, it amuses me now that I was willing to deliberately omit what was, from a personal point of view, the most interesting part of the incident.

Here is the missing piece of the story:

**I was in the truck, head on hand, half asleep, and then I was not. I'll call this instantaneous movement *blinking* from one place to another, for lack of a better word.**

**In this new environment, I stood on an oval dais looking rather intrepid in my bloody and torn fatigues, slouching a bit, dirty and darkly tan, addressing thousands of white-robed beings or personalities. They were arrayed up and all around me as if I stood in the center of a huge stadium, the dais on which I stood being perhaps twenty feet in diameter.**

**The personalities were non-physical in essence, taking on form if they intended to do that for a particular purpose. I perceived the way they looked according to what I preferred for my purposes. At the time, since I had been abruptly transferred from the physical plane, it was simpler to perceive them in a human form, wearing glowing white robes.**

**Most of these thousands were familiar to me, and all were my equal regardless of their admiration for my latest silly feat on earth. (How intrepid is it, really, to choose to get blown up?) I knew the Gathering to be a meeting of many groups representing a wide variety of interests and responsibilities pertaining not only directly to earth and physical universe energies but to dimensions and issues beyond.**

**The concept that I first communicated was that I was tired and had no interest in returning to the physical plane. I understood that the decision was**

3

mine, and at this point my decision was to end my physical existence.

Immediately after that, or perhaps more accurately folded within it, I presented what seems from my current physical body/conscious mind perception to be a transfer of information in the form of an inexplicably complex matrix. The information was minutely detailed and broadly conceptual—at once layered and infinitely dense, yet elegantly simple. It included events, thoughts, incidents, individuals, and groups in all their relationship complexities: stories, concepts, connections, nuances, layers, judgments, and projections. It included kinetic equations and dimensions and symbols and flows. Rather than being a classic life-flashing-before-the-eyes scene, this download was a collection that emphasized what might be very broadly understood as cultural and political information. I was aware that I deliberately offered the condensed data in fulfillment of a request that had been made by this Gathering of personalities prior to my taking on this body for this physical lifetime.

While the personalities digested the matrix I'd made available, I was again amused by the admiration that was sent back to me. They were clearly impressed not only with my Raiders of the Lost Ark appearance but also by the depth and breadth of information I was providing. Yet I perceived the task as an easy one and the information obvious, therefore, unworthy of admiration.

When the thought form or matrix had been absorbed by everyone, which took but seconds, discussions proceeded among the various groups and within the whole of the Gathering. This may seem impossible considering there were thousands present, but it was not. No overlaps occurred, no interruptions took place, no misunderstandings formed, and disagreements were respectfully and thoughtfully engaged and resolved. All communication was accomplished through thought.

They then requested that I return to my physical body to accomplish some further work. I was given to understand that my particular skills with energy were needed at this time and would be effective only were I actually present in a body within the earth vibration. I replied that I was willing, but given my level of exhaustion and disinterest in the difficulties of this particular physical life to date, I requested that certain assistance be provided within that continued physical existence.

While we all digested some details, I retreated to a deep place that I'll refer to as another vibrational dimension, for lack of a better description, where I could recuperate and restore my energies. Other beings assisted with this, doing most of the work while I entered a sort of spiritual deep resting state. From the physical perspective, this state lasted an equivalent of centuries within less than a moment.

When I returned to the Gathering, we agreed upon specific tasks that I would accomplish and specific things that they would assist me with once I was back in the physical. This wasn't a *barter exchange*, as we might assume from our cultural perspective. It was more of a genuinely easy granting of services with no weight placed on the value or relative cost of effort implied by each agreement.

Having agreed, I moved to another vibrational location where healing would be performed on my physical body. From this location, I could see my physical body in the truck, head propped up by my right hand, elbow resting on the door handle exactly as

I'd left it. I could also see my body as an energy matrix. Reading from both those levels simultaneously, I could tell that my right hand was nearly severed at the wrist, my right foot and ankle were badly mangled, and I had a deep wound in my right torso. There was a large hole in my head: I was missing one eye, the frontal sinus, and a portion of my brain.

Some energy beings and I worked together, quickly repairing the body, primarily working through the matrix. The injuries weren't entirely healed, as some were to be of use in situating me for tasks I had agreed to perform or things that I wanted to experience as a whole infinite Self. While we worked, we joked with each other about what should and shouldn't be done and casually engaged in a great deal of goofing off.

When we'd finished, I thanked my companions, and then I moved to another location that served as a convenient jump-off point. There I met briefly with some other beings that were familiar to me. We discussed mechanical details of what I'd agreed to do for the Gathering, as well as some personal issues. Then I simply took a deep breath and popped back into the body.

I estimate that all of the events just described took place in the space of less than five seconds on the physical plane. The truck was still rolling down the road when I opened my eyes. I was aware of a disconnect and had a flash memory of some of what had occurred, but that memory was immediately put aside in order to deal with what was happening on the physical plane.

While this out-of-body experience took place in the past as we understand time, I can revisit the experience, and it is still alive. The scenes and my participation in them retain the quality and details of favored waking life memories or lucid dreams, everything being as vivid as when I first experienced it. An advantage to this lucidity is that I'm able to relive isolated segments of it with a simultaneous awareness of myself in the physical environment. Applying a physical life perspective to what is clearly an environment drastically different from what might be considered normal allows me now to examine and describe deeper layers of the events and environment that are only implied, or ignored altogether, in the short account given above.

In navigating our daily lives, we take for granted underlying structures of culture and environment, and I did the same during the out-of-body experience. At the time I didn't think W*hy am I communicating by thought? How is this possible?* Just as in daily physical life, we don't think *How can I possibly mentally string together words that describe conceptual thought and then make the words audible by coordinating all the correct muscles?* We use physical, perceptive, and cultural tools without necessarily being aware of their origin or mechanics.

Those physical world *base assumptions* are often not brought into focus until we are confronted with a challenge by a different set of assumptions. On a simplistic cultural level, for instance, an American eats pizza with his hands and may not think of that as a cultural choice until visiting Spain where pizza is eaten with a knife and fork. An American might think nothing of a business acquaintance sharing a few details of an impending divorce while a Brit would be paralyzed with discomfort were a colleague to so casually share such personal information (unless it were turned into a witty joke—that British social savior). Some cultures agree to stop at red lights while others consider traffic lights to be less a rule, exactly, than a rather uselessly polite suggestion. On another level, I wasn't conscious of the fact that there were so many muscles and tendons involved in rotating a wrist until mine was shattered, immobilized, and then required to re-learn how to move using appropriate combinations of muscles rather than compensating with others. On yet another level, many cultures assume dreams are not real experiences while others consider them more real than the physical world.

The unconscious or subconscious assumptions we carry around are structures that allow us to interact with each other and the physical world in agreed upon ways, thus making sense of our collective experience. Were I to organize memory according to theme or concept instead of by date, filling out medical history forms might be unnecessarily complicated. Were I to conceive of time in terms of the weather while others used a clock, it might be hard to set up a rendezvous with a friend. Being able to revisit my out-of-body experience while simultaneously being aware of the collective physical consciousness, our shared reality, allows me to bring into focus some of the different assumptions active in each.

The depth and breadth of information available in the out-of-body event is so rich that organization of it in the linear fashion required by writing is problematic. In an attempt to solve that to some extent, I'll begin each chapter with one portion of the story, using that portion as a reference to expand upon. In this way I'll take the reader through the experience more slowly, fleshing out my bare bones account by describing some of the assumptions, as well as my impressions and conclusions, in an effort to better understand at least some basic aspects of the reality that I experienced. After that more detailed examination of the incident, I'll try to bring the information forward in the final chapter, broadly describing how this experience has informed my physical life. After all, we're currently alive and primarily conscious in bodies and a physical environment. If the out-of-body experience doesn't touch that life, its value is limited. Practical application, the manifestation of any experience, is the stage on which we've chosen to learn and expand.

8

# Chapter 2

# The Environment

**I was in the truck, head on hand, half asleep, and then I was not. I'll call this instantaneous movement blinking from one place to another, for lack of a better word.**

**In this new environment, I stood on an oval dais looking rather intrepid in my bloody and torn fatigues, slouching a bit, dirty and darkly tan, addressing thousands of white-robed beings or personalities. They were arrayed up and all around me, as if I stood in the center of a huge stadium, the dais on which I stood being perhaps twenty feet in diameter.**

A logical place to start expanding on a description of the out-of-body experience might be to concentrate on aspects of the environment: the stage, so to speak, within which the actions took place and the personalities interacted. By environment I don't mean simply the location and appearance of the place that I found myself within but also some of the underlying qualities and assumptions that inform and order perception of and within that place.

Though recorded as such, I don't assume that the thousands of personalities actually wore white robes and were seated in a stadium-like setting. When I revisit the experience, I'm able to perceive those personalities visually as points of light in space, sense them as separate energies, or hear them as separate tonal values. I've also seen them as individual crazy-looking monsters and as different animals.

Though happy doses of Percocet could have assisted in coming up with the idea of turning the personalities into monsters or animals, goofing around with imagination began as a sort of game intended to test the elasticity of perception and specific characteristics of the environment that I experienced. The exercise secondarily convinced me of the validity of memory. Although I can alter such visuals as the white robes and stadium, other details of the experience seem to be fixed. If I attempt to alter the tone of the Gathering, the way I look, the information exchanged, or the order of events, for instance, memory will either turn into a static two-dimensional sort of sensory snapshot at the point that I attempt the change, or my mind will go completely blank.

The ability to change some details while others remain fixed suggests to me that the fixed perceptions are *pure*, so to speak. It's possible that the static scenes and blanks indicate mental blocks of some sort, but I don't understand them as such. They belong to portions of the memory that are meaningless: why not allow change to the way I look? To be honest, I would enjoy playing around with making myself more attractive, more dramatic, more dignified. Why can't I make the blood drip, add a dashing hat, pick that twig out of my hair, or change into digital cammies* instead of appearing in the stupid brown BDUs* that are dumpy-looking and lack the wonderfully useful pocket placements of the digitals? Or why not change the gestalt of the experience since I'm a little uncomfortable with some of it? I could match it to others' descriptions of near-death experiences or amuse myself by inserting a few pokes at the more personally embarrassing or regrettable experiments in my life so far while entertaining some suggestions on what to do differently.

But I can't. I can only observe myself trying.

10

And in trying, I'm able to discern subtle differences that exist between the changeable and unchangeable characteristics. Those unchangeable portions carry a deep familiarity, like a mark of authenticity. This is a *feeling* that is not easy to describe. It's akin to the difference I *feel* when closing a hollow-core door versus a solid oak door, or the difference I *feel* when looking at a photograph of Michelangelo's *David* versus seeing it in person, or the difference I *feel* when touching a realistic-looking silk flower petal versus touching a real flower petal. The inalterable characteristics carry a feeling of being alive.

The alterable portions of the environment, in contrast, feel less substantial. They look just a bit more diaphanous, or I sense that they shift vaguely in and out of clear focus. They feel as if they're missing breath.

One understanding of the alterable portions is that my conscious waking mind may have overlaid the base perception with something more comprehensible or acceptable. The thousands of personalities in white robes may be more fully and accurately perceived through some sense beyond what my physical body uses, so without some overlay or interpretation, they would be indescribable or incomprehensible to my conscious mind within the physical environment. Or their being-ness might be more accurately perceived as a smell that I don't enjoy in the physical body (a rotten egg or a decomposing cow), or a visual that I've learned to think is creepy or weird (a cockroach or a slobbering bulldog). Those perceptions would have been a distracting nuisance, focusing all my attention on the revulsion or strangeness. Through the physically familiar tool of identifiable visuals, the overlay may provide a comfortable framework, freeing my attention for more important information.

Like perceptions of time and space.

This Blink Environment doesn't exist in time and space as we understand it. That's not to say that time and space don't exist at all. Rather, they are vastly more complex and interconnect and operate with each other in more ways than that with which we're familiar. Imagine that our familiar time-space is correlated to this book. We experience or read the book in a prescribed way: we concentrate on the printed symbols, reading from left to right, top to bottom.

In the Blink Environment there would be infinite ways to experience the same book. It could be read freely with full comprehension word by word from left to right, top to bottom. Alternatively, the book could be read paragraph by paragraph from right to left, bottom to top, or whole page by whole page in a glance. It could be read from the center out with a progressed comprehension, or it could be touched with the mind and, at once as a whole, understood in a single moment of digestion. It could be read by grouping emotional content: all the tearful scenes absorbed first, then the neutral scenes, then the ones involving joy. Or it could be read from setting to setting, all scenes taking place on the street being read first, then all taking place in a residential structure, etc. The spaces between the printed letters could be read. It could be read from between the fibers of each page, from between the molecules of the ink, or—well, imagine the possibilities. There would be as many ways to read the book as there are points in space.

Similarly, Time and Space in the Blink Environment can be perceived in many ways, existing in what would appear to the physical mind as a dizzying complexity of length and depth, as well as width, and beyond three dimensions. In capitalizing the words Time/Space, I refer to the perception of time and space from the perspective of these non-physical environments, as opposed to lower case time/space which refers to our familiar physical earth definition of time/space.

Within Time/Space resides the choice of limiting focus to our particular and familiar perception of time and space. Our understanding and experience of time and space might be understood as one strand, a subset, of whole Time and Space.

Although the choices and possibilities in what I'll call the Blink Environment might seem chaotic and overwhelming from our physical mind's point of view, any choice in perceptive pathways is simple to accomplish, as is making the choice itself. Consciousness within the Blink Environment is expanded in such a way as to provide a radically and effortlessly broad basis for perception, including an awareness of complex and multi-layered structure and pattern.

In the context described as expanded Time/Space and expanded consciousness, the structure and patterns allow the potential for a full awareness of what we experience in the physical as past and future. Simultaneous experience is a base assumption, presenting no contradictions. As we understand time in the physical, I'm able to talk on a cell phone at the same time that I walk through space as we understand it. While walking and talking, I'm scratching my nose, avoiding running into someone, reading and following the signs directing me to Baggage Pickup, and worrying in the back of my mind about traffic on the way home.

In a similar way, in the state or place of expanded awareness I'm able to simultaneously hold an awareness of my body in the progressive physical experience of sitting in the Land Cruiser rolling down the road after being blown up, and of me standing intrepid on the dais with all its multi-progressive experiences. I am also *outside* both of those focal points while observing them, and am simultaneously experiencing other dimensions not described here.

I'm able to look *at* each of those "me's" and at the same time look *within* them from the outside and *out* of them from the inside. I'm able to comprehend them from within the cells, within the energy, within their (my) perceptive mechanisms, back from various futures, forward from various pasts, or from any other infinite number of focal points. Because Time and Space are multi-dimensional, I am also multi-dimensional. I'm able to perceive from and within any and all of these

13

simultaneously and with varying degrees of awareness as I choose to focus.

And all of the perceptions make sense. Not to my physical, linear, logical mind right now but intuitively and from within the expanded consciousness.

Another aspect to the expansion in perception available within the Blink Environment is an awareness of energies, inert and active, available in the spaces *between* thought. Obviously, that there could even *be* spaces *between* thought implies that thought has form. We're taught that thoughts are private, ethereal (without substance), and powerless until some physical action puts them into force. In the Blink Environment, however, thought is clearly understood as a force in and of itself. Thoughts have form when that is intended and otherwise exist as *energy with potential effect*, though lacking perceptible form. No form of any kind is possible without thought energy to instigate it.

The force of a thought isn't confined to the environment it originates within; the thought permeates various vibrational levels and dimensions. My sense is that thought utilizes energies available *between and within all* thoughts to activate or alter the force of itself, depending upon the intent of the originator. As a concept, the *energy between* is something I can only describe as *potential*. It both exists and doesn't exist at once. Sorry, I know it makes no logical sense. Maybe it would help to think of it as the Easter Bunny, who exists but doesn't exist. Those spaces between are understood and utilized in ways we don't comprehend in physical existence because of our belief systems, just as the Easter Bunny is utilized or not according to our beliefs about Easter, bunnies, eggs, Jesus, candy, springtime, children, resurrection, or hiding objects. (And people think the paranormal is strange ...)

14

Sticking with the Easter Bunny analogy (I may regret this), imagine all the space between the items involved in an Easter egg hunt: the spaces between eggs, couch, table, carpet, ceiling (we're indoors, in case you missed that), fireplace (in the north, I guess), draperies, walls, and windows. Imagine that all the space not occupied by those objects holds—or *is*—active energy. Imagine that the energy is used to hold the physicality of the chair, draperies, walls, and windows in their apparently solid forms. In fact, on the quantum physics level, the space is known to be occupied by energy. The particles that form our apparently solid reality are held together by energy. (In fact, the particles may be energies simply appearing to us as solids, but let's ignore that for the moment for the sake of this illustration.) That energy *between* is an illustration of and perhaps a subset of the energy that I sensed in the *spaces between* in the Blink Environment.

For the sake of this analogy, imagine that the space between the molecules making up the apparently solid object behind which the Easter egg is hidden holds energies that could be used by our minds just as casually as we use a basket to hold the Easter egg. Every thought, drawing upon the energies between, would become a consciously utilized force itself, manifesting or creating whatever pattern or program was within that thought.

That *between* energy is what I sensed being used in the Blink Environment-and in our own environment though without conscious understanding. If we acknowledge that we use those same energies here in the physical environment, our concepts of reality might shift. If we knew how to consciously use and control the energies in the physical, the connections between particles could be tweaked and manipulated at will. The bonds could be weakened, causing a molecule to ooze or bend—or the millions of molecules making up an egg could be loosened, thus causing the egg to ooze and bend until it was as flexible as warm Silly Putty. We could each be Uri Geller, bending spoons at will. Alternatively, the bonds could be

15

organized by thought into a table, a pony, a policeman, or an Easter Bunny. They could be organized to repair our own bodies. It's possible that we could hunt for the Easter egg by shifting our focus to different locations within space instead of shifting our physical bodies, or we could create the egg behind any chosen object by simply thinking the egg into existence.

My understanding is that we do use these energies without being fully aware of it. In the Blink Environment, a wide spectrum of energies, all familiar to us but imperfectly understood, are used as casually as we now toss around the Easter Bunny (so to speak). Until we understand the spaces between what is currently considered physically real and understand thought as energy capable of effect, we're unable to fully utilize the same energies as creative resources for consciously chosen ends in our physical lives.

Leaving the Easter Bunny (thank goodness) and the dizzying potentials of thought as a primary *force of creation* for the moment, *where* is this environment that I experience?

The Blink Environment is less a physical location than an intensity, a frequency, or dimension. It is specific in location yet is not a part of space as we currently define it. Co-located rather than sitting separately above or below our physicality, I could say it sits beside or within or *between* (that pesky concept again), and that would seem more accurate. It touches and accesses other specific realities although it doesn't necessarily have deliberate effect within them. Consider radio frequencies, which exist in the same space within and between each other, usually without obvious interaction.

As a vibrational level, the environment seems limitless, yet its limits are obviously defined within the band of vibrational frequency. My understanding is that an infinity is available within the frequency although that frequency does not offer access to every available potential within every *other* frequency. The vibrational frequency where I received the deep rest healing, for example, offers a largely separate infinity. In some potentials it is unique while other potentials are shared with the Blink Environment. They both contain infinite potential but not necessarily each other's infinite potential.

Every other frequency or dimension cannot be accessed directly from the Blink frequency, or from the deep healing frequency, or from the frequency on which my physical healing took place. Each dimension offers access to various other dimensions while no one offers access to all others. I imagine a sort of latticework or complex network of connections while also understanding that these visuals are only analogies since the reality is so densely layered as to be incomprehensible to my logical mind. Being that there are infinite frequencies, the network is kinetic although some quality within it remains fixed in the sense that once a personality or awareness is familiar with a specific vibration, that state can always be located.

The Blink Environment, like any other vibrational reality, has rules of energy that define structures of experience within it—the rules being cooperative agreements. The personalities or beings that exist or participate in it are aware of the rules and voluntarily create them, maintain them, and operate within them just as we do in our physical world. The accumulation of intent, which is *thought energy*, fixes the laws of that universe more firmly as experience accumulates in the environment. And yet no law is unbreakable; it is only a guideline for shared experience and ever-expanding exploration of the potentials of creative force.

Because we're not fully aware of the laws we agree to exist within on the physical dimensions, whether we're speaking of natural forces or cultural, we're unable to consciously utilize them to an equivalent extent. By a constant, effortless awareness of the rules and the complexities of the structure underlying them, the personalities that operate within the Blink Environment are better able to use the energies deliberately and creatively. As a gross example, in order to use electricity for our own ends, we first needed to understand some of its potentials, limitations, and properties in order to generate it at will and then control what we generate.

The awareness of one's own consciousness within the Blink Environment is obviously broader than what we're accustomed to consider *normal* in our own environment. Through belief systems, present cultures have limited the general awareness of energy systems and the nature of expanded awareness, or ritualized those states through various practices. In the Blink Environment the expanded awareness is free of those limits.

Our perceptions are shaped by what we *believe* to be real and possible within the physical environment. The Blink Environment is fully aware of the dimensions that we consider real and of a myriad of other realities that are not necessarily considered real from the current perspective of our physical reality: the dream landscapes that we visit each night and places we go in moments when we drift off into daydreaming, fantasies, and reverie. Or the blank spaces of those sort of lost moments when we can't think what we were intending to do a moment ago. Or the lost time that we experience driving a car, suddenly coming to consciousness, thinking *Shit, I don't remember a thing between the office and here!*

Those experiences are not throwaways but dips into an expanded consciousness. We slip through time or space as we understand it, visiting the spaces *between.* Instantly forgetting where we were or what we experienced in that missing moment seems to be a function of the conscious mind editing what doesn't fit into its concept of reality. It is the equivalent of my ability to morph white robed personalities into animals.

If our conscious minds were to accept the substance within the moment, our carefully constructed beliefs of how the world works would likely be threatened. *Everything* might have to change: assumptions of what is possible, what is right or wrong, what is good or bad, what is whose responsibility, what is real and not real, what is meaningful, how time moves, how space is organized, how we move through the environment, how we're born, how we die, where we came from, who we are . . .

Stop and think through a few examples of each of those things. Then think of more. *Everything* is a lot of things. Change can be frightening.

(Or is *anticipating* change the frightening part?)

In any case, such change isn't necessarily requisite. We operate within this physical universe as it is currently understood for meaningful reasons. The current limits we've designed are a choice. Whether we choose to change within this universe and how we change and evolve is also a choice.

Awareness in the Blink Environment assumes that our consciousness is the enduring Self and that consciousness is more than what we experience, use, or acknowledge from within the physical environment. The body and our entire physical world is real but is not the totality of the Self's reality. It is not *more or less* real than the places experienced in the dream state nor the places we go between moments. We've been taught to focus and, in some instances, agreed to focus on a narrow band of experience proven only through five physical senses. The comical aspect of that is its implication that what is not sensed through our physical bodies' mechanical system doesn't really exist. We set up our own paradox: if that assumption is carried through to a logical end, whatever is currently out of the reach of my direct sensory perception doesn't exist. If I can't see it, taste it, feel it, smell it, or hear it, it's gone. Just because I can return to it by focusing on it again doesn't prove anything. I frequently revisit the same place in my dreams—yet I'm told that dreams are not real and the place I visited in my dream is a figment of my imagination. If the store I went to yesterday and plan to return to tomorrow is real, so then, too, might be the place that is familiarly revisited in my night dreams.

Often esoteric and spiritual literature flip that conclusion, referring to this physical life as a dream, the illusion. The two ways of stating the same reality focus attention from a different vantage point. *It is all real* solidifies and affirms all experience: that which my physical self is experiencing, as well as the expanded realities my consciousness explores. This is useful to me in bringing the expanded consciousness into the physical consciousness, in blending what my logical, linear mind still often splits into separate worlds. It might be a useful little mantra to try when attempting deliberate out-of-body experiences or learning to bend spoons. It might help in teaching the conscious mind that the paranormal is normal.

*It is all illusion* can be useful in breaking down those same barriers by coming at beliefs from the other side. Saying *it is all illusion* encourages me to detach from the physical reality by suggesting that something I perceive as unpleasant exists as a temporary state within something else, something larger and meaningful. This could be useful in situations that require a re-examination of assumptions about what constitutes good and evil, right or wrong, for instance. Stating the concept either way can be a surprising exercise in expanding awareness and breaking down some of the programming that has taught me to distrust what I instinctively know.

Other characteristics and implications of the Blink Environment are more easily approached through describing other aspects of my experience, so I'll move on to the next excerpt of the account, which will provide a basis for discussing the personalities that I encountered out-of-body.

# Chapter 3
# Personalities, Interaction, and Intent

The personalities were non-physical in essence, taking on form if they intended to do that for a particular purpose. I perceived the way they looked according to what I preferred for my purposes. At the time, abruptly transferred from the physical plane, it was simpler to perceive them in a human form, wearing glowing white robes.

Most of these thousands were familiar to me, and all were my equal, regardless of their admiration for my latest silly feat on earth. (How intrepid is it really to choose to get blown up?) I knew the Gathering to be a meeting of many groups representing a wide variety of interests and responsibilities pertaining not only directly to earth and physical universe energies but also to dimensions and issues beyond.

A problem I encounter in expanding on this portion of the account is in finding a word to properly describe or portray the individuals in the Gathering. Calling them *spirits* might work if the word didn't carry religious undertones of angelic creations or conjure a sort of wispy, ethereal ghostly human form. But it does. *Entity* sounds digital to me, robotic and chilly. The word *beings* is accurate, yet so general as to be almost meaningless and lacking the warm connotation of individual liveliness. I've been using the word *personalities*, and the word comes closest to my feeling about them—perhaps the best I can do with the

21

language limitations. Semantics matter because a corresponding comprehension of the depth of each personality seems dependent upon it. To properly bring them to life through language, I would most naturally call them *people* or *friends*. That would present its own conundrum since they lack a basic requirement of the definitions: our current focus on physicality. For lack of a better choice, then, and having come this far using *personalities* or *beings,* I'll stick with those words and attempt to infuse them with a little depth through further description.

As previously noted, I'm aware of the white robed personalities arrayed around me as I stand on the dais, and I'm also aware of them as energies, points of light, or monsters, as I prefer: an allowance of the environment. I'm also aware of each of them as individuals. Changing my visual perception of them doesn't allow me to change the immediacy of their presence or individuality. They are as real to me as my own hand.

Their number is overwhelming to my conscious mind, yet I'm able to single out any one of them to fully *recognize* the personality of that individual, simultaneously and instantly perceiving and knowing each of the other thousands as unique individuals. That simultaneity of awareness of each of the thousands seems like another nonsensical concept from within the physical consciousness. It's too complex to comprehend. It might help to imagine being in a room full of friends, perhaps at a wedding reception or large birthday party. While listening to one friend telling a story, imagine also being aware of each of the other friends in the room and the ambiance created by the combination of those particular people. Scanning the room, each person is instantly recognized with an awareness of the individual's uniqueness while you are still listening to a friend's story. At the same time, an awareness of the overall mood of the Gathering can be felt: it might be tense, awkward but friendly, quietly content, cheerfully lively, openly joyful, or—woo hoo!—drunkenly raucous.

In the Blink Environment, that simultaneity of awareness of the friend talking *and* friends within the room *and* ambiance is simply expanded to allow one the capability of focusing on *innumerable* points at once with *full* consciousness.

Likewise, the recognition of the personalities through the reading of an energy gestalt of that individual has a corollary in physical experience though it is vastly expanded in the Blink Environment. If you've ever thought of a friend but inexplicably couldn't come up with that individual's name, consider how you knew of whom you were thinking: you may have called up a visual image of that individual, and accompanying that image was a gestalt, or a total sense, of that personality. That *feeling* might have formed over years or within moments, compiled from physical data, memories of shared experience, and judgments of your own about characteristics of the person. Those details are integrated into an idea or a sensed *whole* describing that person as a unique personality. Though you may never have been with a particular friend under some unusual circumstance—after being blown up by a roadside bomb, for instance—if you were to imagine experiencing that incident, you could probably imagine how that friend might react. While your conclusion might originate from accumulated experiences with that friend, you don't consciously and deliberately page through every single thing you know about that friend in order to reach the conclusion. You have a gestalt, one idea unit, representing the friend that you can dip into and come out of almost instantaneously, emerging with the conclusion.

In the physical world, we seem to accumulate the data that informs our gestalt of an individual through experiences within the passing of time. In the Blink Environment, that gestalt is available instantaneously. Being that Time (vs. physical-reality *time*, lower case) is multi-dimensional, the whole of the individual doesn't have to be gathered sequentially from within the linear experience of time and space. The personality's Self exists, complete, in infinite Time and Space and can be experienced whole.

That the personality is, at once, complete is not to say that the personality is static, finished, or unchangeable. Rather, this person is complete within constant creative change and expansion. Assume that a spoken name in our physical world comes to symbolize the whole known gestalt of an individual friend: I'll call her Fiona. That name could be considered an audible symbol of a single complete thought-flash, an idea unit, a concept that identifies Fiona to me. That thought-flash is composed of innumerable individual thought bits while being simultaneously or overridingly one thought: Fiona.

And although Fiona is constantly changing and growing, adding new experiences to her life, her memory, her character, and consciousness—to her "beingness," she remains recognizable to me as Fiona. And although I am constantly changing and growing, adding new experience to my own life through my own shifts, I still recognize Fiona.

Similarly, without the physical visual clues of what she looks like or audio clues of what her voice sounds like, in the Blink Environment Fiona can be sensed as herself purely by *feeling* the energy of her Self, which is a Self that is infinitely richer than a physical world concept of Fiona.

Our culture uses the term "sixth sense" to encompass a broad range of experiences that could be a pale shadow of this *feeling* experienced in the Blink Environment. Extrasensory perception (ESP), telepathy, and other so-called psychic phenomena seem extra-normal (exceptional, para-normal) or fictitious to many within the context of the physical culture and mainstream belief systems but are obviously utilized to varying extents in our physical lives, or we wouldn't have names for them or such extensive examples of experiencing them. Some experience that falls under the designation of *sixth sense* could be a result of hyper-sensitive five-senses awareness to physical clues. Yet many experiences clearly belong to a sensitivity beyond the culturally recognized limits of the physical mechanisms of taste, touch, smell, sight and hearing. The *sixth sense* could be understood as a shadow of much more acute and well-developed sensitivities that are fully available within the Blink Environment.

Like everything else, the action of instantaneous acquaintance within the Blink Environment is initiated by thought and requires agreement between both parties. Once agreed upon, it feels as if I absorb the totality of that personality without invasion or intrusion. The "signature" sense of that unique personality is then instantly and forever recognizable on an energy level. Simply by thinking of that personality and recreating within myself the *feeling* of that signature, I return to be with that particular being.

In some cases, pockets of information within a personality are not in full focus or are not offered. The signature remains the same, but details regarding specific experience or information might be minimized by one or the other in the interaction. As a corollary, in physical life I may talk to John about art and rarely discuss foreign travel while with Jane I don't discuss art, but we talk extensively about foreign travel. Their separate signatures of me would likely dovetail without either being aware of the edits that I impose while interacting with them. The focusing interest of each person minimizes parts of my personality that are not of interest. In the Blink Environment there's an awareness of the capacity and interests of the receiver, and, on the part of the receiver, there's an awareness of that person's own capacity and interests. In a sense, pockets of information are minimized or perhaps skipped altogether when offered to the receiver.

Each of the thousands of personalities interacts by focusing outward a part of Self that purveys character quite clearly: some personalities are all business, some intensely curious, others playful, others quick-witted, sober, or casual. They all, however, emanate a total acceptance, understanding, and compassion. I use the word compassion with hesitation because it carries faint whiffs of pity and hierarchy, the one granting compassion being somehow wiser, more skilled, or luckier than the one to whom compassion is bestowed. Perhaps "co-passion" is more accurate. In our interactions, we were absolute equals without the pollution of competition in any of its myriad forms. The interactions, then, were always with absolute recognition of equality in awareness and a shared passion for *being*.

That absolute recognition of equality and shared passion for *being* underlies every other description that I give of this experience.


To address the interests and responsibilities of the personalities whom I describe myself as being aware, it could be helpful to reiterate the base assumption that, from the perspective gained in the out-of-body, consciousness is assumed as the central and enduring *being, the self.* Physical-world consciousness is a rather exquisitely balanced attention or focus of the whole of our Self on that experience. The Whole Self, as I'll call it, is simultaneously fully aware of innumerable other worlds, possibilities, probabilities, and its experiences within those vibrations or focus points. The other experiences aren't separate from our physical world experiences; the experiences all inform each other, whether we're aware of it or not in our physical consciousness.

All of this is not to say that we are individual and unique beings on earth who will eventually get swallowed up by this big anonymous Whole Self, ceasing to exist as unique at some point. Rather, we are individual and unique beings on earth who are even more uniquely and individually expansive than most of us are now aware. We are more than our physical bodies and the limited minds and consciousness-focus of this physical environment. We are already that Whole Self, perfect, complete, and ever-changing though we may only be consciously aware of a small portion of ourselves.

It was quite obvious from the Blink Environment perspective that it takes specific skill on the part of consciousness to operate effectively in the physical vibrations that we occupy, and not every consciousness has developed itself in that direction. That it isn't exactly easy from an energy standpoint seems to be, conversely and paradoxically, one reason why it can be difficult to remember who we are as Whole Selves while we're within the physical. But the point is this: *all of us* are sharing a unique experience that takes real and amazing skill. We have absolutely no idea how amazing and totally cool we are, really, each of us, and how totally amazing and cool it is that we can maintain a physical body and comprehend experience from within time and space as we do.

This was part of the reason that I received admiration from the Gathering. What seemed quite elementary to me, being familiar with operating within a physical reality, was acknowledged as requiring a high degree of specialized skill from the perspective of those personalities at the Gathering.

The interests and responsibilities of the personalities at the Gathering all, in some way, while not focused within the physical, touch in varying degrees upon this physical level that we inhabit, as well as extend into other dimensions or vibrations.

Taking another sidetrack into language deficiencies, I'm using the term *dimensions* with some frustration. The word carries some sci-fi connotations for me, and—hard as this may be to believe—I dislike almost all science fiction books, movies, comics, stickers, art---you name it—leave me out of it. (Oh wait … I do like the first Star Wars movie, and the Narnia Chronicles were my favorite books as a kid. But really, lose the artwork.) The word also carries a bit of baggage from the hippies and New Agers, triggering—I know, totally unfair of me—visions of crystal worship, dreadlocks, white boys drumming, deeply meaningful tattoos, self-absorbed dramatics, the pale ooze of synthesized Enya and the over-used stench of enough patchouli to gag a rat. (Relax. I like Enya, have used crystals, own a drum, and have engaged in more than my share of self-absorbed dramatics and will continue to do so. I'm just saying … well, re-read the Preface.)

Despite all that, the word *dimension* is attractive in that it signifies, in one use, an *aspect* of something. In fact, my understanding of the various *dimensions*—or vibrations or worlds or focus levels—of expanded consciousness is that they are *aspects* of one encompassing reality. The *one* reality includes all *beingness* or consciousness. It is the endlessly unknowable infinity of creativity and an apparent paradox of infinite numbers of unique individuals that are simultaneously *one*. This encompassing connection is within and of, and creates, is created by, and moves through each unique being, and *is* part of all while also existing separately from what I'll call "All That Is."

This All That Is can be perceived simultaneously as a force and as an individual consciousness that exists within each consciousness and yet is separate from each consciousness or being. It's what might be referred to as God, but the ideas of gods that we have are a pale and incomplete shadow of the All That Is that I perceive. Projecting an idea of a god or gods upon that infinite creative consciousness inevitably limits an understanding of the All That Is in ways that reflect the severely limited comprehension that we have of ourselves and the physical universe.

What I've been referring to so far as vibrational levels, worlds, realities, or dimensions are, in my current understanding, focal levels of consciousness that are as real as the physical world. In that way I understand them to be *aspects* of All That Is, whatever that is—the unknowable totality of conscious and infinitely expanding creation.

Within my very elementary understanding of quantum physics, too, the word *dimension* is appropriate. Physics, I'm told, theorizes a structure for the universe with similarities to what I perceived from the Blink Environment perspective. Our perception of solids is a fiction, as even the smallest perceived particle actually contains no solid whatsoever, and parallel dimensions exist within our reality—dimensions within and beside and between the reality we perceive, which implies probable and parallel experience and realities. In this sense the word *dimension* is appropriate. From now on, this description of its meaning can be applied and used interchangeably with vibration, vibrational level, world, or reality.

Getting back to the point, the concept of dimensions underlies a more specific description of what I perceived to be the interests and responsibilities of the personalities making up the Gathering. While some personalities operate independently, the majority are participants of small groups, each focused on specific interests or tasks within specific environments or focal points. For example, one group's interest involves working with healing energies as they cross over dimensions, which necessarily directly affects healing energies woven through the physical dimension. These are overarching healing energies that exist apart from individual consciousness as a structure of flow. They could broadly be said to inform and flow through healers working from within human form although the energies are specific in that on the physical they pertain to applications that are not consciously practiced in mainstream Western medicine.

Another group's interest is focused on the balance of interaction between points of overlap in dimensions. The overlaps, which could be thought of as multi-dimensional junctions, join dimensional realities (physical and non-physical) to each other. Imbalance within one or between them all can result in bending massive flows of energies, which, in turn, would de-focus consciousness and cause what might be perceived as transmogrification or realignment of creative direction within reality systems.

Another group represents maintenance of energy grids that support laws of energy within and throughout the physical universe that we're familiar with although our current focus excludes a majority of what is actually perceivable. Those energy grids support other dimensional energy systems in ways distinct from, but equally important to, the way they affect the physical.

Other groups work on what we might judge to be more limited levels. One is responsible for assisting consciousness (including physical humans—us) through transitions into and out of the physical levels (like birth or death, for instance). Yet another group concentrates on energy patterns of science within the physical world as we know it, making available specific information that could be intuitively picked up by us in physical consciousness and put to use. Yet another group works exclusively with the energies that create, maintain, and guide cultural systems in the physical world, which could be understood as energy webs that manifest in or are manifested by physical belief systems and social networks.

These are only a few examples, but they offer an idea of the range of interests represented by the thousands of beings. The tasks described presuppose a structure or network of innumerable physical-form vibrations or dimensions, as well as dimensions that function and are experienced purely as energy. Consciousness being present within and throughout all of them, in my understanding, is a prerequisite for their existence and function since consciousness both creates the ever-expanding presence of them and experiences awareness from within them.

The specificity of some of the tasks wasn't held up against what we might consider to be larger, broader, or more complex tasks. Each was recognized as requiring different but equivalent levels of skill and expertise. For the most part, these beings were experts or masters of their fields and, again, "co-passionate" about what they were doing.

The personalities working on these various levels can't be assumed to be overarching governing bodies although that might be a logical conclusion from within our conceptual understanding of structures. They are not some set of saints or gods manipulating realities. What I sense is that the personalities, while experiencing within their own and across many dimensions, could be understood as focused portions of their whole beings just as we are focused portions of our own expanded-awareness Selves. They are not the end or extent of possibility or examples of *advancement* of some kind, nor a step on a hierarchy. They are simply experiencing their own experience, which is distinct from ours, in a sense overlaps ours, *and* is of equivalent value to our own experience. There is a simultaneous infinity of other dimensional structures that co-exist across, through, over, under, and around their own.

My own awareness within the Blink Environment assumes the same expansive understanding of energy and "being" that these personalities exhibit. Some implications of that expanded awareness as it relates to our beliefs, assumptions, and actions in the physical world will be further explored in the following chapter.

# Chapter 4
# Choice, Purpose, and Responsibility

The concept that I first communicated was that I was tired and had no interest in returning to the physical plane. I understood that the decision was mine, and at this point my decision was to end my physical existence.

Immediately after that, or perhaps more accurately folded within it, I presented what seems, from my current physical body/conscious mind perception, to be a transfer of information in the form of an inexplicably complex matrix. The information was minutely detailed and broadly conceptual—at once layered and infinitely dense, yet elegantly simple. It included events, thoughts, incidents, individuals, and groups in all their relationship complexities; stories, concepts, connections, nuances, layers, judgments, and projections. It included kinetic equations and dimensions and symbols and flows. Rather than being a classic life-flashing-before-the-eyes scene, this download was a collection that emphasized what might be very broadly understood as cultural and political information. I was aware that I deliberately offered the condensed data in fulfillment of a request that had been made by this Gathering of personalities prior to my taking on this body for this physical lifetime.

While the personalities digested the matrix I'd made available, I was again amused by the admiration that was sent back to me. They were clearly impressed not only with my Raiders of the Lost Ark appearance but

**also by the depth and breadth of information I was providing. Yet I perceived the task as an easy one and the information obvious, therefore, unworthy of admiration.**

**When the thought form or matrix had been absorbed by everyone, which took but seconds, discussions proceeded among the various groups and within the whole of the Gathering. This may seem impossible considering they were thousands, but it was not. No overlaps occurred, no interruptions took place, no misunderstandings formed, and disagreements were respectfully and thoughtfully engaged and resolved. All communication was accomplished through thought.**

The first paragraph of this portion of my account contains significant implications. Having read other accounts of near-death experiences, I've found that many of them describe some entity or figure stopping them from getting somewhere they wanted to go or telling them that they were required to return to the physical. Obviously my experience didn't include an authority figure directing or curtailing my movements. Whether I returned to the physical or went on about my business elsewhere was entirely up to me.

Having that choice implies to me that free will is respectfully recognized in the environment. I can't explain the fact that others are directed against their will although possibilities come to mind. It may be that those individuals retained some habits of perception carried over from the physical waking consciousness beliefs, and the authority sending them back was either a helper or simply their own voice of the Whole Self, whereas I knew immediately where I was, where to go, and trusted my experience within expanded consciousness. My retention of the form of a physical body while within the Blink Environment might be an equivalent. My sense is that it can take a bit of time for the habits acquired during the physical experience to fade, whether those habits consist of holding a physical form or holding certain thought patterns that pertain to expectations and beliefs that help us function in the physical world. If individuals within the physical experience believe that they'll be met by an angel or saint upon death of the physical body, then perhaps upon death a personality who inhabits the expanded awareness states will appear to those individuals as an angel or saint to offer them guidance. Or perhaps a real angel or saint exists and will meet them. If individuals expect to meet ancestors, perhaps ancestors will meet them.

My own understanding of death as a voluntary transition of consciousness chosen by the individual may have helped shape my experience. Having spent a good portion of my life trusting expanded awareness, I suspect that I may be more comfortable than some in owning myself as more than a series of firing brain synapses. Acting as my own authority, owning that as a law of being, my own beliefs likely shaped or informed my experience. After all, from an expanded consciousness perspective, it's understood that belief— *thought*—creates reality.


When I revisit this scene, the overall ambiance of equality and respect between all participants, noted in the previous chapter, is striking. A hierarchy of power is entirely absent, and no evaluative or punishing judgment is in evidence. Power and responsibility lie within oneself, in one's own explorations of balance and creativity within the cooperative infinity of All That Is, the creative force of all being.

While I was aware of fulfilling an agreement to provide information to the individuals at the Gathering, I felt no sense of judgment applied regarding the way I carried out that obligation or responsibility. No self-evaluation took place regarding whether that had been a favor fulfilled well or executed poorly. It was what it was, and while I was pleased that the information was useful, I was also somewhat indifferent to the effect the information had on the personalities who accepted it. While having communicated some effects of my physical life—I was tired—I didn't judge whether I was tired from doing good deeds or from struggling and failing to reach goals. It felt very much as if the only judgment rendered on my physical life might be my own evaluation of its merits, disappointments, triumphs, and uses.

Although a "life flashing before my eyes" evaluation didn't take place at this time, the evaluative criteria against which my life's actions might be weighed was available. The first criterion was whether my Whole Self, my *Beingness*, was expanded in depth and breadth in regard to understanding the nature of myself within all consciousness. This was closely related to the second criterion: expression of creativity. The third criterion was whether I enjoyed the experience as a whole.

Whether my sense of Self was expanded by this lifetime to date was actually a given, as all experience is assumed to expand awareness of the Self. Whether it added significantly to certain areas or in particularly exciting, unexpected, or novel ways seemed to be the emphasis for my own evaluation. Even in physical consciousness I enjoy unexpected or apparently bizarre juxtapositions, extremes of possibility, and finding things I've never imagined exist. Some of the other personalities present exhibited a structure or emphasis in their approaches to creativity that was entirely different from my own, just as a scientist and an artist in our physical world might approach the same object or action from very different point of view. Some of the personalities were drawn to methodically detailed progression, finding every detail of equal interest. Others were attracted by priorities of emotional intensity while others were attracted by priorities of what I'd describe as cerebral complexity. Preferences in creating and organizing experiences were all accepted as valid. They are

36

simply different paths that lead to the same outcome: enjoyment—the joy of playing with innate creativity.

The realization that enjoyment of an experience is a central criterion for the value of a life surprised me. In reflecting upon this scene, my agreement to fulfill the various requests of the personalities was based *purely* on my own sense of whether I would enjoy the proposed tasks: not *partially* based on my own sense of what would be fun but *wholly*. If I hadn't thought that it would be enjoyable to fulfill the Gathering's requests or that the tasks couldn't be done within activities that would serve my personal interests, I know without doubt that I wouldn't have agreed. And the sense I have is that no one would have minded had I said no. That decision would have been assumed valid and fully acceptable.

*If something is not enjoyable, don't do it* might seem an alarming concept in the context of the physical consciousness we know. Our base assumption, the structure upon which we rest our ideas of self, is that we are basically flawed. If we were free to do whatever we most enjoyed, it's assumed that many would choose to do evil or disruptive, self-absorbed things. Chaos would ensue. What if someone most enjoyed killing people and spent a whole lifetime doing it? What if someone wanted to rape a neighbor, kill a sibling, rob a bank, or stage a coup? What if I didn't want to apologize, or you didn't want to go visit your sick mother. We assume that if set free from social, religious, or and cultural constraints, we'll be freeing base impulses, and those base impulses will likely be bad. Religion tells us we're fundamentally sinners, and science tells us we're fundamentally aggressive survivors. My experience in expanded awareness environments, however, assures me that we're fundamentally good, holy, cooperative, creative, and amazingly cool.

I was hoping to avoid a discussion of good and evil, as I could probably write another whole book in an attempt to explain what I experienced regarding this perceived dichotomy. The subject is fraught with all sorts of cultural and religious baggage that's difficult to untangle, but it seems pertinent to try to explain, very basically, what I sensed about good and evil from an expanded awareness perspective. From a physical perspective it's easy to end up chasing one's own tail on this; I'll try not to twist it into knots.

From the physical perspective, it's appropriate to agree upon limits of behavior in order to create a harmonious collective experience. It may also be necessary because we've built our reality into a structure that discourages or overlooks personal understanding and consistent awareness of our Whole Selves (and so, our participation in All That Is) within our physical lives. Our judgments on behavior, then, are valid *from this physical perspective* and functional *only* within it. We try to curtail the actions of a burglar, a murderer, or a rapist, with good reason. It's a judgment on the physical action, and an attempt to minimize detrimental effects on the general harmony of the physical world, our collective conscious experience.

From expanded awareness *every* action is understood to express creativity, have meaning, and influence the balance and order of the whole of All That Is. From my experiences in expanded awareness, it appears to me that *no being* is considered evil or bad. *Actions* of a being may be understood to be disruptive, inharmonious, or detrimental to the creative flow within any one reality, but the *creativity* of an action could be understood as valid—perhaps even necessary or useful—regardless of the overall disruption. Actions of a being may be understood as likely to look disruptive or evil from within a physical perspective while being considered beautiful, necessary, or valuable creative action from the perspective of expanded awareness and thus *good* in every way.

Here's a simplistic (or simplified, though not necessarily simple) example. From our perspective, we're generally unable to perceive or understand fully the roles that a Whole Self may choose to take on upon entering a body, but from expanded awareness it can be seen that someone may agree to act in a certain way in order to assist others in experiencing something. As outrageous as it may seem to our perspective in the physical, the man who built the bomb that blew me up may have performed that action at my own request. This is not to imply that because it was at my request, his actions are acceptable within the physical world and ought to be overlooked. The role may have been agreed upon in order for the bomber himself to experience what it's like to be chased, arrested, detained, or killed for the violence he visited on others. The bomber's actions don't have to be condoned in the physical world because he and I as Whole Selves agreed to blow me up; we all keep playing our roles within the context of the physical (the collective reality that we as Whole Selves have chosen to focus upon and participate in) according to what we think is good and right.

That as a Whole Being I actually chose to be blown up flies in the face of more than one cultural base assumption. We generally assume that things happen *to* us and that there are many things that we simply *can't* control. Accidents happen, mistakes are made, some people are lucky, and some are not. My experience simply doesn't support this base assumption. Whether consciously aware of it in the physical mind or not, my Whole Self is fully aware of every experience as a cooperative effort between my focused awareness within the physical world, my Whole Self, and other individual Selves. I *craft* my physical experiences. Things don't happen *to* me without my consent; they happen *because* I created, co-created, or agreed to experience them.

Just to complicate matters in one (of many) directions, from expanded awareness, it is understood that beings can become so focused within one reality that they entirely (temporarily) lose track of their Whole Selves. Within that disconnect, they can cause all sorts of disruption through focused but non-cooperative action. This isn't a cause for punishment; it's a cause for healing.

Although in one sense all acts are creative, valid, and good from the perspective of expanded awareness, acts of violence and discord, as well as competition and aggression are not essentially actions that support the best reflection or expression of All That Is. Nor do they express a consciousness of our own inherent goodness or our cooperative connection to every other consciousness. The actions are *out of harmony* with our Selves and the flow of our collective creativity at its *best*. They *diminish* our capability to create a reflection of who and what we really are: co-passionately good and beautiful beings.

We've built our concept of the world on the assumption that humans are basically flawed, and it hasn't given us a particularly attractive world: competition, greed, poverty, war, hate, fear. It has, though, given us a mirror—a world that reflects our collective base assumptions and fears. A physical world awareness of expanded consciousness could assume respect for ourselves and all other beings, manifesting a natural harmony of mutual creativity in the physical world. Until that awareness is common, what we're experiencing now, individually and collectively, is *still* an expression of our Whole Selves in all our profound goodness. It has meaning. It matters, and for our Whole Selves *this* life is creative and entertaining. My Whole Self chose this physical focus and specific culture, and it continues to choose my experiences within them.

This doesn't mean our concept of reality can't evolve into something easier, more harmonious, or more fulfilling than what we have created to date. Life could be shaped into something that *both* expanded and physical consciousness perspectives would consider fulfilling and beautiful. Violence, fear, competition, and other essentially destructive experiences may be entertaining to expanded awareness, but admit it, they're not exactly our best foot forward.

So much for good and evil. I'll move on before catching my tail and gnawing it to bits.

The criterion that I used in judging my experiences intensifies an awareness that I'm fully responsible for everything that I experience in my physical life. In the best of circumstances, my Whole Self and my physically conscious mind would work in concert to shape an experience that an integrated self would enjoy. Physical world base assumptions and beliefs, though, often block an easy expression of the creativity of the Whole Self.

Being that our lives are cooperative endeavors, the Whole Self won't or perhaps is often unable to work through our conscious physical-world beliefs if they contradict its intention. The conscious mind is a creator equal in power to the Whole Self, so its beliefs necessarily shape experience as much as do the intentions of the Whole Self. *Thought creates experience* means that Whole Self *and* conscious self thoughts create experience. In denying the reality of the non-physical and who we are as Whole Selves, we are not only oblivious to our own hand in creating the lives that we lead, but we stand in our own way. In hanging hard onto our beliefs, we are fighting ourselves.

It may be that my Whole Self orchestrated the experience of being blown up, but it could also be that my physical self's beliefs and thoughts are responsible. And if it was an unconscious or subconscious belief that got me blown up, it would have been possible to consciously ferret out the beliefs that supported that experience and change them. It was *within my power* to do that. And without changing the beliefs that invited nearly dying (I'm tired, life is hard and not all that interesting any more, for example), I can be healed of my injuries but would probably just create another opportunity to manifest those beliefs.

41

The *experience follows thought* concept can be applied to anything. If I'm poor and want to be rich, I may be able to ferret out the beliefs that keep me in poverty, replacing them with beliefs that support wealth. My understanding is that the Whole Self is willing to—or perhaps in some cases is *bound to*—bow to the beliefs, requests, and direction of the conscious self focus. It's as if this conscious focus of our Self has taken on a role, and the Whole Self will allow the flow of that improvisation and support it. To the Whole Self, whatever I create will be meaningful, creative, and fun.

Whether it's my physical mind or Whole Self creating experience, there is no *victim status* available. My actions, emotions, and thoughts are not a hopelessly blind product of parents, school, television, abuse, poverty, social prejudice, racism, sexism, or politics. I entered the physical world as a complete being, a full-blown personality, a consciousness with intentions and agreements. My being blown up by a roadside bomb in Iraq isn't the fault of the person who built the bomb, the person who placed it, or the person who triggered it. It wasn't bad luck or coincidence. It was an event that my Self cooperatively created and agreed to, and for my Self the event was and is meaningful, creative, and fun. It might have been unnecessary or avoided had I consciously developed different belief systems, but the value of the experience is not diminished because of that fact.

With this understanding, I may be in unpleasant circumstances, but my conscious mind's joy is understood as a choice that can only be destroyed *by my choice of perspective.* I can choose to view myself as a victim of circumstance or as a creative instigator and cooperative partner. I can choose to view my circumstance as random and meaningless or find and create the meaning in them. My joy need not be destroyed by a self-absorbed colonel, a terminally ignorant administrator, the incessant cell phone chatter of a self-important suit on the airplane, or losing sight in one eye. My joy is destroyed by *believing that they can affect my joy,* thereby making it so. The moment I become aware of myself as a Whole Self, I cease to be a victim of anything. Instead, I become the cooperative creator of my own experience, fully responsible. It's possible to change my trajectory by changing my thoughts.

The wording of that is not meant to imply that I've mastered this perspective in my own physical life. This is not always simple to apply. Consciously connecting to the intentions of my Whole Self is not always straightforward, and beliefs are often deeply seated or otherwise difficult to identify, much less dissolve or change. And certainly changing one's beliefs may sound like an unrealistically simplistic or lame approach to joy for someone starving to death, blinded, or missing limbs—I don't mean to diminish the reality of pain and anguish: it exists, it is real, and it matters. Personally, being in the throes of a migraine or nerve pain or falling down a flight of stairs because having only one fully functioning eye doesn't afford the best depth of field, I'm not wondering how I created this torment and leafing through my beliefs to find the source. I am often, however, aware of and at least slightly amused by my perception of these events as flaws in my life. I'm also perpetually sure that I created the experience, so after the cussing has run its course a quick flip through my beliefs or a little chat with my Whole Self *is* sometimes in order. The differences between the intentions of the Whole Self and the intentions of our conscious physical minds can be a yawning gulf, which can seem confounding if not downright outrageous.

Describing the idea that we each choose our experiences, no matter how difficult or nasty, worries me for the possibility of an erroneous assumptions being made from the statement. It isn't someone's *fault* if they're injured or otherwise have a difficult life. Our cultural beliefs support ideas that consider anything less than an idealized perfection to be a flaw, a mistake, a problem, a lack, a weakness, or the wages of sin. Science tells us that only the strong survive, which then makes sickness, age, or injury an implied threat and, again, a *fault*. Religion tells us that good things happen to good people. It is absolutely essential to understand that, from the perspective of expanded awareness, *all experience is valuable.* So when I say it is my responsibility and choice that I got blown up, and it is others' choice that they have been injured or hurt or are living difficult lives, that is not to be interpreted as placing blame. I'm *not* thinking, *It is my fault.* I'm more likely to be thinking, *It is my unique gift to myself. I can try to appreciate it in some way.*

The staggering variety of our personal lives could and perhaps should be considered fascinating and exciting to ourselves and to each other. Instead of thinking, *Whoa, that person is seriously f\*ed up!* I could think, *Whoa! That experience took guts,* or *That one gets high points for drama,* or *Huh -- very subtle,* or *Shit -- they're really piling it on,* or *Hmm -- they're like a microcosm of the macrocosm of what's going on in the world,* or *I wonder what I'm/they're doing with this? I wonder how it fits into the cooperative whole of creation?* Maybe I can learn from someone else's experience; they may be exploring something that I don't want to go through myself but can learn from vicariously. They may be creating something that I'd never imagined, thus inspiring me.

Understanding things in this way does not negate compassion for suffering and pain. Perhaps paradoxically, it often makes me more sensitive to it. I know that in the intense focus of being in the physical, the pains and discomforts and difficulties are terribly real and can feel endless and utterly hopeless. My own compassion is intense and can be nearly crippling, perhaps partly because I've been somewhere similar but also because I want to be able to wave my hand over the problem to make it disappear, the way I was able to do for myself while out-of-body. I want to give others a glimpse of the expanded perspective that I experienced in order to assure them that their pain isn't forever, there is value and reason in it, and that the reason is their own—the experience is potentially as valuable as their pain is intense and real.

Acknowledging that life can be utterly miserable and difficult, I'm suggesting that sometimes joy can be found even within and between difficult experiences. The way we think about the experience can transform it in surprising ways. By becoming aware that on some level we created this experience and that it's valuable to our Selves, a new perspective can be gained that may shift our emotions and thoughts regarding physical life experiences.

Returning to the Blink Environment—whew! Where were we? Oh yes, we've established that I'm entirely my own authority. I'm free to leave or stay. I'm free to alter agreements, negate them, or enter into new ones. I can disregard my original intent or expand upon it. Within any intent, I can choose one path toward its fulfillment or any of an infinite number of other paths—whichever looks like the most fun to my Whole Self. In the end, purpose is my own choice and that purpose is directed by my personal intent.

Luckily, at the moment I'm in the Blink Environment, so I'm aware that I am profoundly, thoroughly, and perfectly *good*, deeply content, casually confident, broadly compassionate, endlessly curious, and infinitely creative. My disturbing sense of humor, short temper, and irritability with the world as it is has been left behind, so I'm not likely to return to earth to zap the people that I growled at during physical life: obstructive bureaucrats can relax; self-aggrandizing colonels can breathe easy; yo-yo's yapping on cell phones while driving city streets are free of my wrath. To be honest, I don't feel any attachment to the people, the landscapes, or the situations left behind that, from the physical, I might judge as unfinished business. I'm not particularly interested in returning to the physical at all. I'm tired. I wouldn't mind a good rest.

Given adequate motivation though, like maybe the prospect of doing some potentially enjoyable things that I hadn't thought of doing? Tempting ...

# Chapter 5
# Skills and the Consciousness/Body Connection

**They then requested that I return to my physical body to accomplish some further work. I was given to understand that my particular skills with energy were needed at this time and would be effective only were I actually present in a body within the earth vibration. I replied that I was willing, but given my level of exhaustion and disinterest in the difficulties of this particular physical life to date, I would request that certain assistance be provided within that continued physical existence.**

That I could be so easily enticed to return to the physical when I was so exhausted is amusing to me now. I am a bit obsessive about tasks in physical life, too. (I like to call it "directed.")

I hesitate to outline or specifically discuss the skills that were highlighted as useful to the Gathering. I consider them unique and interesting to me because they're mine, but I don't want a description of some of them to be interpreted as grandiose or "special" in anyone's value hierarchy. Parts of our culture artificially elevate certain skills by attributing them to advanced souls, mystics, prophets, yogis, or shamans. Other parts of our culture relegate some of the skills to the trash barrel of psychology—the mentally deluded. Both are distortions of what I consider to be normal perception and

47

universally accessible skills. From the viewpoint of the Blink Environment, we're all a little deluded or deranged in some of our collective beliefs about what is real. It was once assumed the earth revolved around the sun, and if we think we aren't fooled by equivalent certainties today, the ignorant if endearing arrogance of that will undoubtedly be proven at some point. At the same time, we are all shamans, for ourselves and for each other.

A general discussion of skills and values might be more useful to the reader than a description of my particular skills. My experience in the Blink Environment suggests that the skills we enjoy using in the physical are often in some way reflections of the skills of our Whole Selves, or souls if you prefer. Given a choice of performing tasks best suited to a CPA or to an artist, I would most naturally gravitate toward the artistic tasks because that would allow me to act out my Whole Self's favored skills and interests. If I'm a doctor in the physical, that might reflect the interests of my expanded personality in healing, service, or alleviating disharmony within consciousness. If I'm an engineer, that might be an expression of my Whole Being's interests in the mechanics of systems and the manipulation of energies toward specific ends.

It's almost impossible for most us to remove ideas of hierarchies of value, competition, and ranking from our perceptions. Within the physical world, possibilities of variation within experience are endless but are not judged of equal value; their effects are measured against others instead of against the self. From that point we tend to rank people in hierarchies of importance: how many *others* does this *one* affect, how difficult or complex is this job in comparison to another, and/or how many objects does one exercise control over. That assigned value is derived from a framework that doesn't exist in the Blink Environment.

48

From the Blink Environment's perspective, excellence in the expression of a skill is recognized, appreciated, and utilized but doesn't compete. Some individuals may be more adept at maximizing the expression of their skills within certain dimensions, or some may attempt to combine expression of more skills at once than others might do. A few might choose particularly difficult circumstances that limit expression in some way in order to challenge themselves to discover new ways to use their skills; others might choose to develop skills that they don't have a natural affinity for in order to expand themselves in that direction. The possibilities of variation within experience are endless and of equal value to the whole of creation.

It's impossible to be *without effect*, and all personalities experience that which is desired and valued *by themselves*, which is ultimately what matters. Since each self is a vital component of the whole and in natural balance with it, creating something of no value is simply not possible. Someone performing a relatively small task might experience tremendous growth and expansion as a Whole Being while others performing what we might perceive as large and complex responsibilities may be treading water as far challenging themselves. Yet those treading water are having effect, and that effect is of value. One personality might choose to explore a dimension that is completely unfamiliar and in fumbling around there, be ineffective in one sense yet fulfill a personal intent of novel experience; another might return countless times to the same dimension to master completely its peculiarities. All of those are valid and appreciated equally. They are evaluated only by the Self in relation to the Self's intent. The Self is naturally in alignment with All That Is, so that all experience is naturally in support of every other being.

In this context, my own particular skills were thought to be valuable to the various desires or goals of the Gathering, and the intentions of the Gathering interested me in that they aligned with my own interests. The applications proposed for use of my skills intrigued me.

That the skills would only be effective were I actually present in a body appears to have to do with the capacity of energies to interact between dimensions. In order to have effect within any dimension, a harmonic is required on the part of the one attempting to have an effect. Each dimension has its own unique complex of vibrations, which might define the possibilities and limits of action within them. If any personalities don't have or can't achieve a harmonic with a dimensional pattern, their efforts will not be felt within the dimension—the effort will be weakened, distorted, or pass between what is perceived as real with no effect. If one can achieve a harmonic with the dimension, the action undertaken will have effect on the dimension, and the effect can be as clean as the individual's skill and intent allow. The action might be perceived to bend or turn an energy flow, strengthen its general direction of flow or a specific current within it, or might radically alter it.

Earlier I described the interaction between dimensions or vibrational levels at junctions and locations of overlap. All dimensions are connected in what could be visualized as a network, yet no one dimension offers direct access to every other dimension. This can be kept in mind in relation to effectiveness of intent/action from within or outside of the physical dimension: effect can be achieved from dimensions that intersect or overlap, but those effects might be diluted or limited depending on various characteristics of the dimension. Working from within a dimension affords a greater range of effect.

As an example, imagine a meeting of six or eight close friends. The conversation develops a natural flow, supported by a complex symphony of—at the least—shared feelings (you all like each other, though probably for different reasons), shared memories (you know quite a lot about each other's lives—some more than others), and collective learned behavior (cultural rules and norms of social interaction, assumptions about what is real, what is meaningful, etc.). Now introduce a cat. The cat walks into the room and sits beside the couch looking at everyone, thinking cat thoughts: *There's a mouse in the corner of your kitchen.*

No one notices the cat—or the mouse. The cat is occupying a space that is overlooked in the interaction between the friends because of their focus. Even though the cat is there, fully aware of all of the friends, physically existing as (supposedly) solidly as the people, it doesn't have enough in common to have an effect on *these* people in the *present* moment. The cat is the equivalent of an overlapping dimension, missing full integration of a close harmonic. The cat is in harmony with the mouse dimension but overlooked from the human dimension.

Now another human friend walks in the door, and, bristling with excitement, she interrupts the flow of interaction by shouting that she saw a mouse as she came through the kitchen. She notices the cat and says, "Cat! What are you doing?! Go eat the mouse!"

The tone, flow, and ambiance of the room changes instantly. This friend has interacted on a close harmonic with the group reality, partly by being a fellow human which made her announcement easily communicated. So although her news is unexpected and might even seem alarming to some of the friends, being far from anything they imagined would enter into the moment, it *is* perceived and her effect will have ongoing influence. This woman is in a close harmonic with the group, and because of that, she's able to introduce a new element and shift the flow of energy in the room. She has also

51

brought to attention an overlap in the dimensions of human and cat/mouse.

As a more compact example, imagine music being the equivalent of a dimension. Music is effective for us only within the range of human hearing mechanisms. There are infinite notes available in all dimensions, but for physical effect in the physical dimensions, the notes must be within the physical range. Bringing it back around to the cat, what is audible to the cat is not necessarily audible to the humans, yet enough of their perception lies within shared ranges that they are able to interact and affect each other.

In the physical world dimension, as in any dimension, an appropriate energetic harmonic has to be matched to a degree that affords interaction. That is not to say that one has to be in a physical form to have any effect. In the context of the music metaphor, sounds that are not audible to us have been shown to have effect. Similarly, effect can be achieved without a physical form, but some influences are most easily achieved on the physical dimensions by entering into a physical body— by participating. By doing so, an overlap will be extensive, allowing for potential of the most intense effect.

So my skills are recognized and requested, and the reasons for applying them from within the physical dimension are understood. But hey, I want some assistance if I'm going to return to the physical body. Already tired, going back into a body that was just blown up might mean dealing with a lot of inconvenient limitations and distractions that sound like a tedious bulk of unpleasant work. Fresh from the physical, I'm clear on how difficult it can be to manifest experiences and situations that are fun for the physical body and mind— which can be disturbingly different from the Whole Self's idea of fun. Frankly, I'm not all that interested in flailing around in that sort of place again.

From the comfortable perspective of the Blink Environment, the physical life could be imagined as the equivalent of our watching a movie. While it's playing, we immerse ourselves in it, accepting the premise, sharing the emotions, and caring how the conflicts conclude. When the movie is over, we snap out into "real" life. Although emotions might linger, we know that the movie was not "real." No one really died. The city wasn't annihilated. The creepy monsters won't crash in through the living room wall. The movie's plot perhaps conveyed messages or lessons or held personal significance or meaning, which we walk out of the theatre now owning—if it didn't, we probably thought it was a dull movie—so the experience mattered. It might even be revisited in memory or in another theatre. The ideas and emotions were fun or informative. They were valuable. But we don't consider the story real.

In some sense, the physical lives we're living now look that way from the Blink Environment. The experience of living is considered invaluable, meaningful, and fun; its pains, struggles, horrors, difficulties, anxieties, and frustrations are not dire at all. From the Blink Environment, it's easy to minimize or ignore the things I consider difficult because I know the ending and the ending is always good. I always walk out of the movie theatre. In that sense, those things that drove me nuts in the physical are not real or lasting. From inside the physical moment, experiences can feel almost impossible to bear while from the Blink Environment they're perceived to be of a moment's duration—valuable, amusing, and lacking the emotional charge.

A child falls and scratches her knee—just a little scratch. She cries and runs to her mom. The mother kisses the knee, laughs, pats the girl on the head, and goes on about her business, knowing the child is fine. *It's nothing, just a little scratch.* This vignette describes my perception of our lives from the perspective of the Blink Environment: all our anguish and trials are nothing much. No matter how dire, difficult, horrible, wrenching, heart-breaking, painful, or long-lasting they are to us from the perspective of the physical—which *is real,* they *are* all of those—the experiences are still just little scratches to our Whole Selves.

Being fresh from the physical world and only moments ago blown up by a roadside bomb (of all things), I retain the vivid reality of the physical consciousness perspective. Are you kidding? I'm exhausted from it, and I haven't even started with the blast results yet! So while I am in the deep contentment and confident amusement of my own expanded awareness, the immediacy of that expanded awareness allows me the vast relief of knowing my physical life problems are *just scratches.* Yet I am still quite clearly aware that what appears as a scratch to the expanded consciousness can seem long, painful, difficult, tedious, and unpleasant to my consciousness in the physical world, and I don't like it.

I'm willing to return to the physical, but I want some assurance that it's not going to be returning to endless tedium or dire difficulties. I'd like something that's as fun for the physical body and limited consciousness as it will be fun for the spirit. Would *you* have allowed this opportunity to pass by unaddressed? I think not! I'm not always right on top of things, but I caught this one. It's all very well to enjoy the movie, but I don't see why I can't also enjoy being *in* the movie. And personally, I don't like horror films. I don't think being scared is fun at all. I don't always find that being emotionally twisted, stretched, and wrenched is enjoyable. Terribly sad movies are not relaxing and fun for me. Juvenile humor, unimaginative characters, or predictable dialogue is dull—I don't like to be bored. Quirky love stories, complex mysteries, adventure or action stories with happy endings and a lot of witty humor lightening up any film are big hits with me. Obviously I doubted my own ability to create and maintain consistently enjoyable experiences from within a physical existence. So I proposed that I get a little assistance with the more mundane, dull, painful, and unpleasant aspects of life.

Have I gotten that assistance? I'll return to that subject in Chapter Nine.

In the meantime, I'm about to blink to another environment.

# Chapter 6
# R and R

**While we all digested some details, I retreated to a deep place on what I'll refer to, for lack of a better description, as another vibrational dimension to recuperate and restore energies. Other beings assisted with this, doing most of the work while I entered a sort of spiritual deep rest state. From the physical perspective, this state lasted an equivalent of centuries within less than a moment.**

**When I returned to the Gathering, we agreed upon specific tasks that I would accomplish, and specific things that they would assist me with once back in the physical. This wasn't a barter exchange, as we might assume from our cultural perspective. It was more of a genuinely easy granting of services with no weight placed on the value or relative cost of effort implied by each agreement.**

Having proposed practical assistance for the trajectory of my physical life, should I ultimately agree to return to one, I move to a place specifically suited for rest.

Again, there is no guide or outside direction involved in getting where I want to go. I seem to know exactly where to go and *blink there through intent.*

Looking at the experience now from the outside, it seems as if I fold in upon myself, turning inward until I am completely enveloped by myself. Rather than taking me into a smaller reality though, it's as if I turn inside out, emerging into a different but equally spacious place. Within it, I am without boundaries. As a consciousness, I'm unlimited, enormous, with no edges or definition. This limitless space appears at first to be dark. The darkness isn't impenetrable though. It's rather what I imagine deep space might be like: it's as if darkness itself contains all light and has depth that can be sensed and seen. It could be described as a sense of *potential* light— remember the Easter Bunny?

The stillness and vast space is profoundly peaceful in its silence. Although the idea of a vast emptiness might seem cold and intimidating to some, this vastness is intimate and cozy. Imagine burrowing under thick down quilts in the most comfortable bed imaginable while a snowstorm rages outdoors. Close your eyes then, and while you are feeling so physically cozy, enter into the limitless dark, peaceful, and creative space of the mind. Imagine the body as weightless and without boundaries within that, and the deep contentment that I felt in this Rest Environment might be approximated.

This interlude in the Rest Environment lasts one moment *and forever.* I can sink into the state now and feel as if I've always been there and am able to stay forever if I'd like. I still drift there, suspended, for long periods, yet come back out of it to find only two or three seconds have passed on the physical plane.

The Rest Environment feels like a different dimension than the Blink Environment. I want to describe it as being on a different thread of Time/Space outside physical form dimensions. It may not be possible to create physical form in this dimension; whereas the Blink Environment has variations of physicality should one choose to work with that. This thread, actually, feels as if it is *deeply private*, as if it may not be accessible to anyone at all without my guidance and permission.

Once in the depths, I perform what might be a variation of the life review that others have reported upon returning to the physical from near-death experiences. No deliberation is involved, meaning that I don't settle in and say, "Ok, bring it on." It's more of a casual drift into reflection, the way we tend to drift into sleep with images smoothly flowing through. And whereas in a sense my life flashed before my eyes, it is not a flash so much as a deep and multi-layered, instantaneous yet leisurely wander through life. I simultaneously perceive layers of emotional, mental, and physical experience with underlying connections and patterns and progressions, as well as the links between all of those. Layers and links that we don't acknowledge as real in physical consciousness become obvious. Coincidences are revealed as connective tissue between deeper aspects of the intersections between self-consciousness and physical experience. Interlocking patterns of my connection with all consciousness became apparent. *All consciousness*, including other people, mass events, objects, animals, plants, elements, what we perceive as individual molecules, atoms, subatomic particles, and energies. Although we arbitrarily assign consciousness to only a few things in our current definition of what is real in this physical universe, it becomes clear in the expanded consciousness perspective that all form has consciousness. And all of consciousness cooperates to co-create and maintain what we think of as our physical world reality.

These perceptions are available visually, but the impossible depth and richness is an experience of multi-sensual absorption, a digestion and integration that our language has no adequate words to use to describe. A simultaneous awareness exists of the interconnectedness of innumerable strings of being, expansion, possibilities and probabilities, back in time and forward, sideways and between what we perceive from the physical. The multi-layered digestion and integration includes alternate paths of action, reaction, and interaction as they may have played out had I chosen this or that option instead of what action I did choose to follow at any point in physical life. Those are perceived as explorations, like dreams within this Rest Environment that inform the actions and movements that I did choose through focus to follow or inhabit.

The process of review is not analytical since it isn't linear or evaluative in a way that we might understand from within a physical consciousness. The experiences are absorbed through all levels of comprehension and perception at once. The senses of perception feel as if they are expansions of the physical senses we use on earth though more closely connected to each other. If I hear a sound, it is much richer than anything imagined in physical experience. At the same time that I hear the sound, I am also able to taste that sound, to feel it, and to perceive it visually. So in some way, a single sense is all senses, each informing the other. The physical senses that we use could be likened to a thin and isolated strand within a thick cable while the expanded senses would each be as large as the whole cable with each braided into the other sensory cables so that any input immediately flows through all cables.

Upon integration or more accurately *within* integration comes a deeper comprehension of my life experience as it relates to all that I am—my expanded consciousness as a whole—and to All That Is, the creative force that is within all that exists on every dimension through every consciousness. Evaluation takes place only in the sense of deciding whether this or that *maximizes* Whole Self potential, whether through it I am able to absorb a broad swath of connective experience, or whether it serves as a contraction in some way. I'm noticing whether my experiences carry through intent toward exploration in particular directions, which were personally determined prior to having entered this particular physical experience. The life is evaluated, then, on the basis of whether it is especially useful toward personal creative ends and whether it is particularly useful in moving forward into other creative endeavors. Within that, all experience is recognized as essentially good.

This idea of goodness was addressed in Chapter 4, but it is worth noting again. As an example of the goodness implicit in every single experience and the meaning of judgment when applied within that base assumption, imagine that you have a big bowl full of all the types of candy you particularly like. In judging which you want to eat next, in other words which is important, you don't find a single piece that isn't interesting, attractive, and enticing. How will you choose which one to eat right now? It's hard! But let's say that you just had a chocolate bar an hour ago, so you'll take chocolate off the list for now (I know, that's not a very good reason to forego chocolate … it's just an example). You like looking at some bright yellow pieces and the way they contrast with the other candies so you won't eat those yet; and you had jelly doughnuts for breakfast, so something squishy isn't as interesting at the moment as something crunchy. All the red peanut M&Ms—perfect! You sit there and pick out all the red peanut M&Ms, contentedly munching away.

All of those pieces of candy are good, just as every single experience in life is good. The evaluation, or judgment, on the choice of candy or on the life experience, is only applicable in light of personal interest or intent, which shifts and changes easily depending on this or that subjective circumstance and interest. The decisions aren't dire and excruciating because every choice has a good ending (even though in the *physical* experience, it might be excruciating, boring, painful, or ugly). Choice is not fraught with tension and fear; every choice will lead to creative and satisfying experience.

From the Rest Environment, everything is valuable, yet some choices could be understood to offer more interesting views along the way or to offer a distinct value (the clarity of key lime pie vs. the symphony of chocolate). A small action might be unexpectedly found to be a lead toward interesting possibilities never before imagined. Chords of experience become formed during integration and evaluation. I'm able to see all the ways that small actions affect interconnections throughout the physical dimension and beyond into other dimensions, rippling outward without my knowing (from the physical perspective) that one action could have such far-reaching effect or that it could result in that particular effect. This life review might more properly be called a life exploration, as it was an exercise in discovery more than evaluation.

The exploration is accomplished with great amusement and affection for the self for *being*. The belief structures of karmic law or religious punishment have no place in this process or in fact in my entire experience. Even now I can return to these states and in looking for such structures, find them only within the physical dimensions as structures created and maintained purely by the very belief itself: thought taken form. The beliefs are not cosmic law or rules under which the expanded consciousness operates because consciousness exists already beyond them. Consciousness can simply slip between those ideas or step past them.

All of this activity may not sound particularly relaxing or restful, but within it I felt deeply relaxed and peaceful. A lack of time limits, criticism, fear, anticipation of punishment, recriminations, debts, outcomes, or conclusions is profoundly liberating. The overall ambiance is one of radiant, quiet, sound, profound joy. Not joy as a reaction to something but the joy of *being*.

As described, I was not alone in the Rest Environment. The others that are with me are working on technical adjustments while I go about my own business. Present at my request, I understand that these beings are experts at healing on these dimensions though they seem to lack any emotional involvement in the process or with me personally.

Their work implies that I have some equivalent of physicality though I perceive myself as a limitless consciousness. It's as if, as energy, I yet have some interior structure. Within an ethereal no-form, I contain an infinite depth of energy structures that have no form and occupy no space. If these could be perceived as visible patterns of living, they might be constantly changing shapes. I sense them as mechanical structures of perception that assist with creative experience and integration. This might be thought of as an equivalent of the physical body structures that support the mechanism of the body: circulatory or lymph systems. The technicians were only tinkering with balances in these systems and structures as if tuning a car or changing a light bulb. My translation of the adjustments is that they aid in the functioning of consciousness as a whole at top performance. Important or essential in that process, they have nothing to do directly with information or the quality of consciousness itself.

When I feel sufficiently rested, I return to the Gathering in the Blink Environment. Being outside time and space as we understand them, no disconnect or lapse exists between the time I retreat to the Rest Environment and the time that I return to the Gathering. Describing it as a progressive experience and laying it out in a linear fashion for the sake of making rational sense out of it, unavoidably distorts it. I could more accurately say that while standing in front of the Gathering proposing assistance from them, I shift focus to a simultaneous experience in the deep Rest Environment.

As introduced at the end of the last chapter, I request that I receive assistance once back in the physical. From all I've described so far, it might seem that I should be perfectly able to affect my own assistance with physical experience since I'm an expanded consciousness with such broad awareness available. Upon thinking that, however, I find a flood of conceptual information describing the difficulties involved in accomplishing these tasks once back in the physical focus and thus, the advantages to having outside assistance. The intense focus currently used to maintain the Self in what appears to be a consistent physical form within what appears to be a consistent physical universe in conjunction with the belief structures of physical consciousness (what we call our minds) can make it difficult to maintain full comprehension of who we really are as expanded beings, and even if we remember that, to effect the conscious consequences. Whole Self intentions can quickly veer off course under the influence of the conscious mind in a physical universe. Beliefs taught to us since birth and ingrained through the benign brainwashing of repetition via collective consciousness—which provides the structures of reality that we currently perceive as real—have influence on and can affect or even block the Whole Self intentions. Though beliefs can interfere with clear expression of the Whole Self, the Whole Self will still inform the physical existence to the extent that the conscious and subconscious minds allow.

I introduce this concept here but will not go into it any more deeply. A whole book could be written on the implications inherent in it. What is important to carry forward is the awareness that assistance can be sought and obtained through intent.

While seeking help in obtaining or experiencing specific items or events in the physical world, I also request assistance in maintaining a degree of Whole Consciousness awareness when I return to inhabit the physical mind. Given enough pressure from culture, I might find it easier to give up and go along with the prevailing concepts of reality instead of retaining and reinforcing what I know to be true. It's easy to lose track of the Whole Self and what is real when we're repeatedly told that what we know is nonsense. Our cultural belief systems don't support the fact that expanded and enduring consciousness is our natural environment, present *and useful,* within the physical.

The specific events or objects that I requested assistance with can be described as falling under the category of removing what amounts to practical irritations and limitations. As an example, everyone has challenges in life that seem to repeat in various disguises. Let's say someone, a kind-hearted and wonderful person, has a chronic shortage of money. This person might suddenly obtain a lot of money but immediately receive a lot of bills, thereby negating that financial advance. *What the ... ?!* (We've all been here, in one way or another.)

Keeping in mind that *form follows thought,* not *thought follows form* as we've mistakenly taught ourselves, the bills that eat up the wealth are actually a manifestation fulfilling some conscious or unconscious beliefs of that person.

Let's look at an example. Chester wants to be wealthy. Old Chester thinks of himself as a pretty good, mostly ethical, very moral, quite generous, generally normal sort of person. Having been watching the news lately, he's come to believe that rich people are unethical, mean, greedy, ostentatious, and arrogant. Being a Christian, old Chester also has a little niggling voice inside that says he might not get into heaven if he's a wealthy man because though he's not as big as a camel, he's definitely bigger than the eye of a needle. Being a businessman, Chester also believes that supplies—the earth and everything in it—are limited, which would mean that if he hoards too much money, someone else will have to go without it. A kind, generous, moral, ethical person on his way to heaven wouldn't be comfortable with that.

Well, in order for old Chester to maintain his morality, ethics, generosity, and kindness, then, he sure as hell won't allow himself to become wealthy—because then he would be immoral, unethical, greedy, stingy, and he'd have a heck of a time getting into heaven.

I call these sorts of simultaneously held beliefs *contraries* and certainly have my share of equivalent patterns. That sort of repetitive challenge is, frankly, boring to me. I expect to be able to address the pattern in myself that creates that kind of experience and move on. Of course, physical consciousness is not always so straightforward and cooperative! The contraries are often buried in physical life's base assumptions, which can be hard to find. With the sources of those patterns being more obvious from the Blink Environment and knowing that my own full awareness of the Blink level wouldn't necessarily come easily to me once back in the physical body, I suggested that the personalities in the Blink Environment remind me by tossing unmistakable hints, clues, or reminders in the way of my physical mind, and even complete an outright erasure of some of the contraries prior to my returning to inhabit my physical body.

In relation to that, as everything exists in relation to everything else, I requested assistance in expanding my physical mind awareness so that I would approach life more consistently from at least a simplified version of the understanding I carry within other dimensions. Among other things, I hoped that this might assist me in manifesting skills that could be quite entertaining on the physical planes: maybe I could levitate, for instance (come on, admit it—it would be fun!). If my awareness of what is possible held a memory of at least some of the expansion experienced on other dimensions and applied that to the physical universe, I was pretty sure the next fifty years of life in a physical body would be infinitely more entertaining than the first fifty years had been, encouraging me to stick around to accomplish those tasks the Gathering had requested I perform.

Between those two themes, I felt as if I'd thoroughly addressed all my physical-world problems. Aren't I clever!? By retaining an understanding that everything experienced on this dimension is a creation of cooperative and individual intent, I would be reminded to alter my intentions in order to eliminate pesky challenges or to at least find the value (or humor) in whatever enters my life. Remembering that energy is used to create and maintain this illusion of a solid universe progressing in one direction (ideally forward) through time/space, I would perhaps be able to erode some of the limiting belief systems that I've accumulated regarding what is real and what is possible: remnants of religion, theories of current science, and various cultural limitations. Once rid of those, intent might be freed to explore paths beyond and including such popular pursuits as affording a dream house, traveling to Peru, or buying a cool car (white Porsche 911 Turbo, thanks). Those are all quite attractive goals in certain ways and ultimately attractive to me, not as ends in themselves but as tools to use in enjoying and validating an exploration of the creativity of *experience* played out on the physical stage.

What I was requesting from the Gathering was—and is—reminders to keep me awake to the enduring Self, the consciousness that is one with all other consciousness. I asked that, should I get wrapped up in the illusion that our universe consists of solid physical objects, I be nudged awake to remember that our universe is energy, which is created, maintained, and manipulated by intent. Which is simply thought.

# Chapter 7
# Healing & Assistance

Having agreed, I moved to another vibrational location where healing would be performed on my physical body. From this location, I could see my physical body in the truck, head propped up by my right hand, elbow resting on the door handle exactly as I'd left it. I could also see my body as an energy matrix. Reading from both those levels simultaneously, I could tell that my right hand was nearly severed at the wrist, my right foot and ankle were badly mangled, I had a deep wound in my right torso, and there was a large hole in my head. I was missing one eye, frontal sinus, and a portion of my brain.

Some energy beings and I worked together, quickly repairing the body, primarily working through the matrix. The injuries weren't entirely healed, as some were to be of use in situating me for tasks I had agreed to perform or things that I wanted, as a Whole Self, to experience. While we worked, we joked with each other about what should and shouldn't be done, and casually messed around with a great deal of goofing off.

The dimension from which the healing of my physical body is performed has a close harmonic to the physical. Whereas in the Rest Environment reality is entirely energy and in the Blink Environment reality is an infinite choice of either physical manifestation or pure energy, the Healing

Environment has a vibration that necessitates form without dictating its structure. It resonates closely with our own physical universe although the structures of physicality are expanded. The Healing Environment feels as if it exists specifically as an extension of our physical universe, an analogy being that the Healing Environment is like a balcony or catwalk above the physical world as we know it. This viewpoint affords a more complete picture of what's going on in the physical in direct relation to the Whole Self, the natural state of consciousness. From that expanded awareness and while in very close proximity to the physical, access to tools that illuminate and directly influence the physical are available.

By "working through the matrix," I mean that we worked with the structures that organize energy into the form of a physical body—in this case my body. We normally think of healing the body in terms used by medical science, which is a mechanical manipulation of physical organs, bones, fluids, and other parts. From the Healing Environment, the whole of the physical body appears somewhat ethereal because it is all seen as what it is: organizations of energy. The spaces that exist between and within what we perceive as particles, the spaces between the particles that make up an eye or a bone or the skin, are obvious. The energy structures that organize and hold the energies in their physical form are visible, appearing as a complex matrix. That matrix is what we manipulated in order to repair my body's injuries.

I haven't previously discussed the fact that within all of these non-physical environments, any physicality that I retain is uninjured though my physical body sitting in the Land Cruiser is severely damaged. The enduring being that I am, retaining what I perceive as a sort of shadow of physicality while in the Blink Environment, is a perpetually healthy, flexible, and comfortable form. If I think of this as equivalent to an age in a physical body on earth, that age would be around thirty or thirty-five years old.

70

I call the form a "shadow" because it is somewhat ethereal looking and is so clearly *not* solid. The form is, at this point, more a leftover habit of intent than it is deliberate. As kids we used to do something that can be used to illustrate this idea of a shadow habit: stand in a doorway with your arms at your sides. Lift your arms out to the sides until your wrists and hands are pushing against the door frame. Push hard with your arms for about one minute, then let go, and step out of the doorway. Without your applying any effort, your arms will rise out to the sides as if gravity were no longer in play. That tension left in the muscles could be thought of as a *shadow* of their more deliberate push against the doorway. The form I retain in this expanded awareness environment is an equivalent: a habit of mind, a shadow of the mental tension it takes to maintain physical form in a physical environment.

Being so fresh from the physical dimensions, within the Blink Environment it felt as if deliberate concentration would be necessary to lose that shape or form quickly. The vibrational proximity to physical earth reality naturally supports the habit. Merely blinking into other environments of pure energy, like the Rest Environment, effortlessly sheds me of the physicality due to the different vibrational level, which doesn't allow for a physical form.

The physical age equivalent, this particular thirty year old form of my body, might be seen as optimal and most natural. It's the inner image that requires the least effort to maintain, like a default image of my physical self. An old woman I know once said, "I'm older now, and don't resemble myself as much as I used to." I imagine that inside herself she still felt thirty years old and looking in the mirror she recognized that this aged body did not resemble her *Self* as much as it did when she was young. Perhaps we all feel that way as our physical bodies age. I suspect any of us who have what appear to be permanent injuries or illnesses that change the way we look or move can attest to the fact that *inside* we are always whole and healthy,

71

as consciousness, as rich personalities, as creative, healthy beings within a physical form.

Although I've described this Healing dimension as a variation or extension of the physical, I don't have the sense of any personality solely inhabiting this Healing Environment. The specificity of the environment makes it useful to enter at certain times only for certain actions. The personalities that I interacted with are not *constantly* within a physical form or *conscious* from within a physical form as a *normal* state in the way that we've situated ourselves in our world. The physical form is created upon entry, and entry into the dimension is a matter of shifting consciousness and vibration within the Self. A personality only becomes physical, to some degree, in the sense that the rate of vibration necessary to maintain a harmonic is slow enough that it approaches our physical universe to the point that we, in our bodies, could physically perceive the personalities in certain instances. From physical reality the energy of their being might be visually perceptible as a filmy, amorphous shape, or they could easily organize their energy into the configuration of human form or into any other organized form, should they choose to do that. In this sense, it is not unlike the Blink Environment.

What is distinct from the Blink Environment is this closer connection with our physical universe. Interaction with our physical dimension from the Blink Environment touches someone living a physical life on the level of thought or consciousness. The vibration of the Blink dimension doesn't allow for direct manipulation of what we perceive to be physical "solids." On the other hand, the harmonic vibrational level natural to the Healing Environment intersects much more closely with our physical universe. Manipulation of physical solids is easily accomplished through working the energy matrices.

As an example of these distinctions, from the perspective of the Blink Environment the influence on the physical could be likened to having a phone conversation with a friend. You can exchange ideas but aren't able to hug, nudge, poke, tug, or otherwise physically move each other around in the environment. From within the Healing Environment, the energy of thought can move the physical directly.

Two personalities work with me in the Healing Environment. Although I don't know the personalities as physical people in the physical world, within this environment one of them is familiar as an old friend. The ease and humor that we bring to the activity is intimate with the quick communication and inside jokes common between friends or colleagues who have known each other for many years. The other personality is more of an observer, as if learning how to do this work and having to apply some effort to keep up with us.

No essential difference is evident between these personalities and those of the Gathering in the sense that they are all perceived as complete beings, individual and fully aware of themselves and All That Is—the Infinite Creative Force and Consciousness. Put into immediate terms, they all feel like personalities that, should they focus into a human being, would not stand out at a dinner party. I don't perceive them as unknowable or unrecognizable in the way of a sci-fi alien monster or a being who doesn't share some significant overlap of consciousness with us. Our natures are similar: we are consciousness. Differences exist in demeanor, interests, styles of interaction, preferences and things of that nature, but basically we are of one shared awareness. As distinct individuals, in the way that we as humans remain basically aware of the shared experience of being human, we share the basic awareness of being conscious. Not all of these personalities encountered in the various environments have had experiences in the human physical form. Not all of them have chosen to participate in this particular reality. Our interactions

73

and recognition of base similarities come from the expanded awareness state rather than from shared background or experience in the physical earth universe.

Although the familiarity is obvious from within the expanded awareness state, from within our physical consciousness state some of these personalities might seem frightening or as lacking in consciousness altogether. We don't normally recognize the consciousness of an electron, or a table lamp, for instance, though they do contain consciousness. Some of the personalities that I encountered in these environments seem somewhat cold, robotic, lacking emotion from a physical human being point of view. Yet they are clearly living, conscious beings and related to me as a living, conscious being. It's recognized that we exist in concert, all experience being cooperative and parts of one source: All That Is.

That primary awareness of the inherent relatedness of all consciousness is not necessarily something that we focus upon within the physical. How others are different from us tends to be more noticeable than how they are like us. We make value distinctions in describing the consciousness of animals or plants as opposed to ourselves and judge many objects as inanimate. We group people from different cultures separately from ourselves or separately categorize people with different clothes or skin color. Because we don't normally recognize many forms of consciousness and their enduring similarity, we concentrate on distinctions between forms. Even in thinking, *Well, we are all living beings,* we don't include all consciousness in the assumption; we ignore the table, computer, sidewalk, the wind, a stone. We often don't interact even with other recognizably conscious beings from an innate respect for their inherent value as *beings*. In that oversight, we set up separation and competition rather than recognize a natural alike-ness that would support full awareness of our cooperation.

Our distinctions are revealed to be artificial and look arbitrary from the perspective of expanded consciousness. From the perspective of any of these expanded environments, aggressions, irritations, intolerances, defenses, and competitions common to physical mind consciousness—and so, our physical lives—seem laughable. The fact that my physical body is blown up within an international conflict involving tens of thousands of beings provides an amusing basis for the goofing off and laughter between us as we fix my body. The conflict, any war, isn't judged as good or bad from criteria of expanded consciousness. The violence is a little baffling and considered an odd "physical-world phenomenon," but it's also entertaining to watch the multitude of conscious beings navigating it as a unique and creative experience.

If physical experience is understood as an equivalent to our going to a movie, the movie will only be absorbing to the level that our individual minds allow or choose to participate in the illusion. Imagine that I watch one of the dinosaur movies from the 1950s. It's impossible for me to buy into the illusion of the movie and become emotionally involved—I'm laughing too hard at the technical aspects of such primitive special effects, the stagey acting, and the practiced accents that sound vaguely Etonian. It all strikes me as hokey and hilarious. This is an equivalent of observing our physical dimension from the Healing dimension. Watching the movie, I can easily see the reality behind the illusion. While appreciating the creative efforts, cooperation, and application of acting and technical skills within the context of the time—1950s—I maintain my viewpoint of early twenty-first century. Likewise from the awareness of my Whole Self on the Healing dimension, I appreciate the physical world with all its amazing creative efforts, cooperation (largely unconscious), and skills applied to exist and experience within it while it remains an illusion and is highly amusing. I can see the reality behind the illusion.

As described earlier, the healing action itself is accomplished from the level of the energy matrix and is nearly effortless. With a focus of intention, *heal this*, and an equivalent of waving a hand past that portion of the body, the body is restored. The action isn't dire or heavy with self-conscious weightiness, technical intricacies, or drama. Within ongoing amusement, a thread of intention is held, and that intention moves the physical reality.

As we heal my body, many of our specific jokes and amusements might not seem funny or even make sense from a physical mind perspective. We joke about the specific and intricate timing necessary to pull off being at exactly the right place at the right time to be blown up and the vast networks of agreements between people that are necessary to make it work in just the way it did. We find it quite funny that all involved in the incident experience what they think is the same incident, yet each individual splits off into his/her own string of reality so that his/her perceptions of the details of the incident will never match. (This is a concept that I'll discuss in Chapter 9.)

While healing the body, we try different combinations and extents of healing, laughing at some of the combinations as we imagine possible consequences and challenges each would present in experiencing a continuous progression into the future within that body. We try making my physical body fully blind and find that to be very funny as we project challenges I'd be likely to encounter as a result. We try a complete healing of my head, arm, and foot, leaving only some small shrapnel in my arm, and laugh at how many people would attribute such minor injuries to luck since others in the truck are maintaining much more extensive injuries. We try leaving part of my skull missing and moving shrapnel into the brain to cause brain damage, then watch, laughing, while a trajectory of a life with that challenge takes shape. We try removing my right hand altogether and fall all over ourselves laughing while watching me trying to learn to write, eat, and otherwise lead with my left hand.

These variations on the healing still make me laugh, but that doesn't mean I'd think some of those situations were at all funny to actually experience on a daily basis from within physical consciousness. In describing this scene I have some fear, as I did in Chapter 4, of unintentionally minimizing the genuine emotions and difficulties that exist as a result of the IED* incident that I was in, as well as others that I know of, or inadvertently insulting others whose difficulties in life might be current, intense, and raw. The emotions and physical extremes encountered by others who were in the truck with me, who were in the teams that helped get us out and patch us up, the families whose lives have been irrevocably altered by this and many other equivalent situations are *real*. And some of the stories are heartbreaking when viewed from within our physical universe ... we are currently living from within this physical universe, after all.

In order to understand the humor, it's absolutely necessary to adopt a comprehension of the body and physical life as temporary and the soul or spirit or consciousness as enduring. Were I to publicly express my amusement at some of these sorts of situations in others' experiences, I'd likely be judged as rude and heartlessly insensitive. Until a broader consciousness is more common, laughing at or ignoring anyone's pain and discomfort will be considered insensitive because it most often is: it tends to originate from ignorance, arrogance, or self-defense rather than from understanding that we've each, as an expanded consciousness, *chosen* our experiences *as they are*. Perhaps only when we recognize a co-passion for *all being*, a delight and joy of having chosen to experience *this* situation from within *all possible* situations, and awaken honest admiration and curiosity for others' unique experiences will it become socially acceptable to ignore or laugh about pain and discomfort—our own or anyone else's.

Until then, it will be difficult to find amusement within some of our most intriguing creative endeavors.

While fooling around healing my body in the Healing Environment and being fully cognizant of some of the tasks I'd agreed to perform for the Gathering, my companions and I also more seriously explore what scope and type of injuries might best situate me in fulfilling some of those tasks.

Chapter 4 carried a discussion of my own responsibility in creating and agreeing to participate in this whole incident. That sense of responsibility is also implied in the selection of my injuries. I chose the injuries; I crafted my experience. They are not a result of coincidence or bad luck and aren't a punishment from some god. A common base assumption, particularly prevalent in religious belief systems, is that if I'm a good person, good things will happen to me, and the natural follow-through: if I'm a bad person, bad things will happen. A Catholic friend of mine once told me that she couldn't understand why someone she loved had died because she thought she was a good person, and she had always believed that *bad things don't happen to good people.* Her base assumption said that somehow we earn and deserve that death of a spouse, that car accident, this illness, that impossible boss, this crazy stalker, or getting blown up. Even New Agers and "enlightened" eastern philosophies support this base assumption through ideas of karma: what you put out will come back to you (seven-fold, in some cases). If bad things are happening to you, you must have acted selfishly or meanly; you must have sent out negative thoughts or done something nasty in a past life that you'll pay for now.

My choosing which injuries to retain and my being blown up by a roadside bomb in the first place are assumed to be valuable, useful, and good from the perspective of my expanded awareness states. The experience isn't a punishment for actions or thoughts that were bad or evil and isn't bad luck or a mistake. My injuries are not reflections of some construct of original (or even mildly quirky) sin. From the expanded perspective of my Whole Self, the event and aftermath are experiences that I chose for various reasons with amusement and a sense of joy and excitement for this novel experience. That I'm not always as thrilled about the results from within the physical perspective as I was when I dreamed up this adventure often strikes me as amusing even within occasional frustration or discomfort. (In the meantime, getting blown up is a great source for jokes…)

In the end, we settle on a particular level of healing for my physical body that will serve my wants and needs.

I'm ready to return to the physical.

# Chapter 8
# Jumping Off

**When we'd finished I thanked my companions, then moved to another location that served as a convenient jump-off point. There I met briefly with some other beings that were familiar to me. We discussed mechanical details of what I'd agreed to do for the Gathering, as well as some personal issues. Then I simply took a deep breath and popped back into the body.**

Like the others, this final environment is more a state of focus than a place, and this state feels as if it exists between the physical dimension vibrations. If the physical can be thought of as a chord, this environment would be a vibration between the notes of the chord, within the chord but separate from it.

The environment lies between the solid physical and pure energy matrices, between physical mind and expanded consciousness, and between the time and space of events on the physical plane. Nothing of particular effect is accomplished from this environment. I'm aware of—but not manipulating—the physical world. I'm aware of—but not communicating directly with—personalities occupying places like the Blink Environment. It's a waiting place, a location specific to returning to a physical body. Revisiting it now, I feel as if I stand within the scene of the blown-up truck while it is suspended in time: a very *Twilight Zone* sort of feeling.

The beings that I meet with on this level have a very practical awareness of consciousness operating within the physical dimension. The joking and fooling around that takes place here is more sober or wry in deference to understanding that what looks easy and fun from expanded awareness can be difficult and painful within the body and can seem endless once immersed within the time/space construct. The discussions we have with each other remain focused on very particular events and situations. The mechanics of setting particular energy levels from within the physical dimension and then different ways of maintaining and directing the energies toward desired goals are discussed in depth and in relation to the unique mental and emotional habits of my physical-focus personality.

Whereas the discussions on the Blink Environment were, for the most part, broadly thematic, the discussions here are more nuts and bolts. In the Blink Environment we are architects. Here we are the construction contractor. Once back in the physical body, I'll be the grunt pounding the nails.

In this environment I'm fully aware that once back in the physical body I can, at any time, choose to veer from the original intent of the Whole Self. From within my conscious mind I'm free to choose not to participate in an event or situation with no punishment, imbalance, or ill effect. I may choose to direct my life from preferences of my physical life consciousness, or relax and let the Whole Self lead. I'm free to become more aware of the Whole Self and act from a more integrated perspective with the Whole Self and physical consciousness working in close tandem. My perception is that any of those options are equally valid and acceptable and depend entirely on each individual.

Nine personalities are with me in this environment. All nine are intimately familiar. Some people or ideologies might refer to these personalities as guides, and some might perceive them as guardian angels. My own perception is that they are friendly and adept personalities who voluntarily fill a particular role that includes guidance, protection, and assistance. They maintain a broad focus and offer a "touchpoint" for me while I maintain the intense focus necessary to function effectively within physical existence.

Their skills are equal to mine while their viewpoint from outside physical reality allows them to assist me in ways that would be particularly difficult to replicate were we all working from within the physical realm. These personalities are able to project trajectories and thereby assist me with avoiding unexpected clashes, physical threats, or side-tracking off the broad course of interest intended by the Whole Self. I think of them now similarly to the way I thought of my personal security detail (PSD) in Iraq: my energy-level PSD team. In Iraq we were accompanied by an armed PSD guard team whenever we traveled off the base. They gathered intelligence prior to travel, planned routes, drove the armored vehicles, and guarded us while we inspected construction sites. My energy PSD team maintains a broad view of interactions, scopes out and advises my subconscious or unconscious toward productive routes, and guards me against unexpected intersections of experience. In addition to PSD-type duties, these personalities offer advice, run energy errands, and offer support, ultimately at my own direction and request. As equals, they are friends and colleagues, similar to friends and colleagues on the physical plane who help us think through decisions, offer a perspective we might miss, and watch our backs when we need that. They are full support without being directors. If I were to say, "Don't help with this—I want to do that on my own, even if it takes me a long time to figure out within the physical environment," then they would stand back and watch (probably falling all over themselves laughing. They seem to have a tendency for fond humor that is only really funny when firmly fixed in an expanded consciousness perspective. This can be a little irritating ...).

Although in this scene we don't affect the physical environment in any way, these personalities have the capacity to affect the physical in many ways. Appearing to have few limitations, they can influence thought patterns, create situations or coordinate entire events, enter dreams, temporarily take on a body, or communicate with me through an audible voice or visual flashes. They are able to manipulate physical energies in ways that would be perceived by us as moving solid objects or even creating them.

About fifteen years ago I was walking a dog named Mesa through a residential neighborhood in Tucson when suddenly a pit bull rocketed out of an open door across the street. The pit bull ran full speed straight at us, and I thought, *This can't be happening. There's nowhere to go.* Mesa and I froze. In that instant, a car came speeding down the road, seemingly out of nowhere. I hadn't heard it coming though the car was souped up, and the road was long, straight, and quiet at that time of day. Timed perfectly, the car sped right between us and the pit bull, which then ran smack into the side of the speeding car with a loud thump. The car disappeared down the street, and the pit bull staggered back to the doorway from which it had come. The whole thing happened very quickly, within three or four seconds. Mesa and I looked at each other blankly, Mesa actually let out a big sigh, and then we just continued our walk.

That perfectly interfering car could be understood to have been created by my friends or guides. The whole incident may have been orchestrated, or it may simply have been a stray event. Dimensions or probabilities may have overlapped in an unexpected way that posed a threat which would not have served any of us and so was better avoided.

The only limitation that I perceive in regards to the actions of these personalities, and the limitation is voluntary, is that they always act in support of the intentions of the individual that they're assisting. Acting out their own personal creative intentions through manipulation of the personality they're assisting is not in their operating procedure. Their creative intentions are focused and directed toward support of the particular physical personality—in this case, me.

All of these personalities have lived within physical bodies and have a workable understanding of physical existence. Some of them simultaneously live within physical bodies at the same time that they act as energy PSD teams. Although this may seem impossible or confusing to our minds, we accomplish similar things in our daily lives, as described previously: we can discuss a business problem on the phone with a colleague at the same time we fry up a couple of eggs, and at the same time we monitor in the back of our mind what the kids are doing. We multi-task. As a Whole Being of expanded consciousness, the personalities are simply able to simultaneously focus fully on what we in the physical might consider to be much more complex groups of tasks. They are able to maintain a constant awareness of my life and simultaneously conduct their own life or lives without strain.

The simultaneous life they experience could be within the same physical-time era that we're currently participating or in what we would perceive as the past or future. This idea of being aware within the past and/or future is possible as a function of expanded Time/Space, as well as being complicated by probable realities and infinite dimensions. The nature of expanded Time/Space is such that all that exists already exists is forming and is potential at once.

From our perspective, if our future already exists at the same moment that our present exists, free will might be assumed to be negated. Infinite probable realities and dimensions assume free will, however. Continuous and continuously expanding, possibilities require infinite individual choice of focus and infinite on-going creation. An awareness or existence within what we would consider to be our future doesn't mean that it's the same future each of us would focus within during the present experience of individual consciousness. It is only one of an infinite number of probable futures. Choice is active and vital.

One example or application of that understanding of futures would be that psychic readings, ESP, and similar predictive practices are a reading of probabilities. The skill required to follow one thread through infinite probabilities seems mind-boggling and might offer perspective on why even very good psychics often appear wrong in their predictions: perhaps they followed one fork while the current collective consciousness followed another. Some psychics are probably more adept at tracking the most likely paths of manifestation or focus available to an individual, so their predictions and readings appear to be very accurate. Some may be adept at understanding and reading the intent of an individual Whole Self's chosen focus, thereby recognizing the strong likelihood of a person choosing to experience one probability rather than another. Some psychics are likely more adept at discerning the trajectory that cumulative physical consciousness to date is leading toward, regardless of the intent of the Whole Self or in discerning the path that mass consciousness is leaning toward.

The mind-boggling complexities of probable and parallel realities that I sensed within the expanded awareness states hint at other possibilities, as well. The inviolable nature of free will and the fact that every thought has profound and deep influence, for instance, suggests that simply giving someone information on their probable future affects the trajectory of infinite consciousnesses. It may cause that person to choose to follow a different focus, thereby making it appear that the psychic's reading is incorrect.

I'll leave the reader to contemplate other possibilities within an infinity of probabilities and return to this subject in Chapter 9.

When I'm ready, I simply shift attention to my physical body and focus my intent to return. This is as easy as it is for us in the physical to glance up from this page.

*Pop.* I'm in the body.

I'm back in a Land Rover, now charred and blood-spattered, rolling silently down the highway in Iraq.

# Chapter 9
# The Application of Impossible Things

*I think from where we stand the rain seems random. If we could stand somewhere else, we would see the order in it.*

~Tony Hillerman, *Coyote Waits*

Unfortunately, here in the physical world I can't heal my body with a wave of the hand, "blink" my physical body to another environment, or even remember fully my Whole Self's purposes and interests. What is incredibly simple and readily understood on the expanded consciousness levels often seems impenetrable and incomprehensibly complex from within physical life. From my current perspective, existence beyond the physical is utterly lovely, delicious, and strange, infused with limitless love, richly fulfilling, and euphorically effortless. It's beyond entrancing, and I'd honestly prefer to be there.

Yet this physical life is a unique experience, and *it* is entrancing from the perspective of expanded awareness. It is utterly lovely, delicious and strange, challenging, and wildly exciting. The razor focus required to remain in the collective physical is intensely satisfying for the Whole Self. Physical reality is a balancing trick, a performance high, an intensely concentrated speed test of complex skill sets. We're each an F-22 pilot flying fifty feet off the deck through an impossibly narrow canyon. Finding myself in the unusual situation of having been blown up, I felt as if I were flying that jet fifty feet off the deck through the narrow canyon *upside down.*

In contemplating a return to the physical, while still a little tired inside and knowing I'd immediately be immersed in what could pretty accurately be described as wreckage, I was *excited*. Fresh from experiencing the ease of Time/Space, probable realities, experience as a result of thought, free will, and personal responsibility, healing through intention, life as fun, blinking from here to there, nothing as solid, everything as conscious, individual and yet one with all ... focusing on the physical again looked thrilling.

While I rarely feel that pure thrill from within physical focus, remnants of it certainly inform my perceptions, as do all elements of my out-of-body experience. It may seem that knowledge gained out-of-body is not really practicable for use within the lives we lead. Yet the information is already put into practice whether we acknowledge it or not. Expanded awareness necessarily coexists with and constructively informs physical life.

In case the reader feels cheated to have bought a book based on being blown up in Iraq only to find a disappointing dearth of blood and guts, I'll try to make it up to you in the next few pages. A description of the physical world that I returned to participate within seems a useful touchpoint to use in addressing the application of expanded consciousness to physical life—and fair way to wrap up this book.

I'll remind the reader that definitions of military slang can be found in the glossary.

Here, then, is the full text of the account written as an exercise in keeping memory true and honest while I was still an inpatient at Walter Reed Army Medical Center. This is the physical world that I returned to.

**I had just closed my eyes, hand propping up my head, elbow on the door handle. It was the end of a long day of construction site visits, and now only a few minutes out from base. I'd long ago quit paying attention to what was passing by outside the window**

and lost track of how far we were from the rest of our security convoy. This team seemed to travel with a half kilometer or more of road between wagons, and I hadn't seen the IP* escort for awhile. Not knowing the two security men in the front seats well, I hadn't chatted with them. Some men prefer to rivet their attention on the environment; they weren't talking with each other, so they might not welcome questions or comments from me. The team was running on closed mic*, a stupifyingly dull way to travel in the back seat of an armored Land Cruiser, cut out of the chatter of hyper-aware security men informed by multiple sets of alert senses. As a passenger, I'd hit the familiar point of being artificially lulled into boredom.

All I heard was a "pop" ... the sound of a champagne cork from one hundred meters. The Microsoft sound of opening a new window. A finger snap from across the office.

I vividly remember taking a long, deep breath—more of a sigh that echoed an internal sigh. I thought, *Shit*. I was tired inside, exhausted from long days spent trying to train a new project manager while catching up with a demanding workload after an insufficient two weeks of leave. I didn't want something hard, something that would require effort. I wanted to rest.

Tough luck.

*Get on with it*, I told myself.

I opened my eyes.

I wasn't able to see out of my right eye, the one my hand had been covering as I'd settled for a short nap. My left eye was fine. I let both hands rest on my thighs. Both were covered with blood. *Such a beautifully saturated, vivid color*, I thought, *that alizarin crimson*. I lifted my right hand back up to cover my eye.

91

The inside of the Land Cruiser was charred looking, smoked with powder burns or whatever it is in an IED* that causes that black toasted look. There was blood all over. I looked over at Ben [colleague] and said his name at the same time I noticed a hole in his thigh. The femoral artery should have been there, I was sure, but he wasn't bleeding. *Perhaps the hole had missed the artery*, I thought, even knowing that was impossible.

Ben moaned loudly. 'Shit,' he said. 'Oh shit.' He rocked a little, bending forward and sitting back up. He didn't respond to my voice. I touched his arm, but he didn't look at me.

*He can't hear me*, I thought. He's panicked. *Let it go for now.*

We all sat straight in our seats, then, the vehicle rolling straight down the road, and after Ben stopped moaning, it was dead silent.

The truck rolled for what felt like a couple hundred meters, then made a perfect and silent turn to the right, rolling off the road onto a clear area of sandy dirt. I didn't see Ian [our driver] move, but it was such perfect control—he must have been conscious and steering.

The truck stopped.

I put my right hand back down on my leg and studied it again; the skin was completely shredded on the little finger and ring finger. The skin was all there, just pocked with holes like a parmesan cheese grater's surface. The other fingers weren't so bad, though the whole hand was bloody.

It felt as if that took a long time, and now when I relive the moment, it was slow and leisurely. It felt important to take in what things looked and sounded like, to assess the state of this new environment. In addition to the eye and hand, my trouser legs were soaked in blood, though I couldn't see any holes in the fabric. My legs and feet felt fine, and they were still there. I optimistically made the assumption that the blood came from one of the others.

No one else was moving, so I thought I had better. I started to lever myself toward the center console. My right wrist wasn't working properly. I quit using that arm, putting the hand back over my eye.

Moving in what felt like full consciousness but slow motion, using my left hand for leverage, I maneuvered myself onto the center console, twisting around from the waist to face the front of the truck.

I was looking for the transponder, but there wasn't one. That probably didn't matter; one of the other trucks had to have seen us get hit. If they hadn't actually seen it, they would notice our radio silence; they would see the distinctive vertical black column of smoke rising straight up into the air. They would know. They were on their way and would have radioed base.

I tugged at the med kit* next to Mark's feet, but his legs were jammed against it. I had no strength to pull and no leverage. I gave it up. I think I tried to pull Mark's long gun* out from between the med kit and his legs, but that was jammed, too. Now I'm not so sure—did I try to pull his long gun out? Maybe. Maybe not. Why didn't I take his handgun? I didn't think of it. It was not a priority at this point—to be armed. I didn't hear any small arms fire or additional explosions that might have indicated a coordinated attack. I was sure the rest of the team would come quickly to help us.

I looked at Mark and Ian in the front seats only long enough to determine that they, like Ben and I, weren't bleeding out. Were they conscious? What were their injuries? I don't know. I didn't focus on that. Maybe I didn't want to know, but I'm not sure it occurred to me.

I unclipped Ian's seat belt, hoping that would help get him out more quickly when the team showed up to help us. I can't remember unlatching Mark's, but maybe it was the other way around. *Remember to unlatch Ben's*, I told myself.

I pushed myself off the console, turned, and sat back into my seat. By that time, I had forgotten to unhook Ben's seatbelt.

I leaned back and looked out the window.

The glass had a film on it. On top of the thick ballistic glass, the film made it difficult to see out, and without my glasses, I couldn't see well out of my left eye anyway. This frustrated me. It had to be my right eye that got hit—that eye had good long distance vision. My left eye was nearsighted. I had to turn my body at an acute angle to gain a fuzzy view behind our vehicle. I couldn't see the other trucks, only desert.

I looked back at Ben. He appeared to be unconscious and still wasn't bleeding. An Iraqi face appeared at the gun port on Ben's side, which had had its cover blown out. The man was in uniform: one of our Iraqi police escorts. His eyes were huge when they met mine.

'Help!' he shouted, turning his head toward the back of our vehicle as he did it.

*So the team is pulling up behind us*, I thought. He looked at me again with those huge, frightened eyes, then disappeared.

I looked down at my legs again, BDU's* covered with blood. I lowered my right hand and looked at it, skin chopped up on my fingers.

I heard a shout and Ben's door jerked open. Jack appeared, leaning in to look at us.

I leaned forward a little and toward him. 'I'm ok,' I said urgently. 'Get Ben—his leg is bad.'

'You're O.K.?' Jack asked.

'Yes,' I told him. 'Get the others first—I'm ok. Ben's leg is bad.'

I think other men from the team came then, behind Jack. Someone cut Ben's seat belt, reminding me that I'd forgotten to unhook it. *Shit*—I leaned over and tried to unsnap it, but by the time I found the release button, they'd cut through the belt and were pulling Ben out, laying him on the ground.

Ian was next. Men helped him out of the front driver seat. I couldn't see where they took him. I tried to look out my window to see how the trucks were deployed and where we were, but all I saw was a patch of nearly bare ground, dirt, and a Land Cruiser with no movement. None of the men were visible.

My own door was pulled open. 'You okay, Nat?' Jack asked.

'I'm ok,' I told him.

'Let's see your eye,' he said. 'Move your hand.'

I lowered my right hand and watched his expression, which didn't change. I thought that was probably not a good thing, but he didn't toss cookies and he didn't start yelling so maybe the eye itself was still there. Finding out wasn't a priority, and I immediately moved on mentally. Jack reached out and plucked the remains of the rim of my sunglasses out of my brow—it felt as if it had been imprinted into my numb skin when he plucked it out. 'Okay,' he said, handing me a bandage. 'Hold this over it.'

I held the bandage against my face, and he helped me out of the truck. When I put weight on my right foot, I stumbled, pain stabbing up through my heel.

'Okay?' he asked again.

'Okay,' I told him. 'Just my right heel.' I hopped, keeping weight only on the toe of the right boot. It didn't hurt that way.

He helped me to the center of the ring of trucks and told me to lie down on the ground, take my helmet off. I lay down on the ground, took my helmet off.

I rested my head back against the dirt and relaxed, wondering where everyone else was. I was glad to be lying on dirt. I liked touching the ground, the warm desert sand and grit. I took a deep breath of the warm air and studied the blue sky. The hot sun felt good soaking through my clothes. I wondered why they pulled me out of the truck before they'd helped Mark because I could have waited until they helped him. I was conscious, not bleeding. I wondered if it was because I was a client, technically their first responsibility or something. I hoped not and was glad they'd helped Ian before me. The sky was a beautiful blue, and the dirt was warm, familiar, comfortable. It was so calm and quiet where I was.

A few minutes passed before someone came to get me, told me to come with him. I remember wondering where everyone else was—*a team of at least a dozen* *men, the IP\* escort—where were all those men?* I wondered if they were deployed around our perimeter, working on Ben, Ian, working on Mark, manning the radios ... at the time I thought *I should be seeing some of this activity,* and I couldn't figure out why I didn't, why it was so quiet and calm where I was.

The man helped me hop to a Land Cruiser, and he placed me in the back seat. I forgot my helmet, leaving it lying in the dirt.

I knew most of the men on the team by sight, yet for some reason I paid no attention to individuals as they helped me. I was only aware of good, competent men helping, taking care of business. For some reason Jack was the only man that I recognized during this whole event, the only team member I remember speaking to aloud after I'd spoken Ben's name as we'd rolled silently down the road just after the blast.

I remember thinking, *These poor guys,* suspecting that the men on this team, the ones who walked away, might have a harder time dealing with this for awhile. They would have to go on in the same environment, doing the same things, taking the same risks but now with a physical memory of helping fucked up people after a hit. They would be in the same environment but with their minds and emotions changed. I would be occupied for awhile in healing. I would be busy with something new, in a new environment, captivated by the moment, however shitty that moment might be. If I could, I wanted to let them know that I was ok and that they did all the right things, all that was possible to do. I told myself that once things stabilized, once I arrived at Walter Reed or wherever I was going, I would find a way to tell them how grateful I was and how much I respected and loved working with them today and for the past fifteen months.

97

Ian was sitting beside me in the truck they'd moved me into. We looked at each other. He signaled something to me, but I didn't understand. He did it again, something to do with my eye, or his eye, or the bandage I was holding to my eye, or one he needed for his eye. I shook my head, confused. He tried again. I didn't understand. I turned away to look out the window, frustrated. I was embarrassed for some reason, for us, for my not understanding.

Now I can't figure out why we didn't just speak to each other; why I didn't just speak to him. I suppose he started out not speaking, and since he was signing without speaking, I followed his lead. Now it seems absurd. Hey Ian, what were we doing? Now it amuses me, two people who could talk perfectly well signaling incomprehensible messages at each other ... I can't help laughing as I write this. *What were we doing?!*

I stared out the window then, though, frustrated, embarrassed by my dense inability to understand, wondering what he wanted, trying to decipher it. And still wondering where everyone was. No one was visible outside the window, just a couple of static Land Cruisers. No men, no movement. Nothing was happening. Just dirt and stationary trucks. Desert. Sky.

It felt as if we sat there for a long time. Now I think it was five minutes, not much more and maybe less.

*What has been accomplished by this?* I thought staring out at the desert. *What has changed now for anyone, having blown us up? What has been moved forward or resolved? Nothing. It's utterly empty. This is how violence is profoundly pointless.*

The radio was on open mike ... 'We've got two superficial, two critical,' someone said.

I remember thinking, *Mark is the other critical.*

'Correction … two superficial, one critical,' the voice almost immediately stated.

And I knew Mark had died.

I don't know why I knew it was Mark. It could have been Ben, couldn't it? His femoral artery was gone. But I knew it was Mark.

I wondered if I'd be blind in my right eye. I wondered if there was some advantage to that, remembering a dream I'd had after my grandmother died. In it she was blind. She made beautiful pictures in my mind and told me in a very intense voice, 'Natalie, you don't need eyes to see.'

*Maybe if one eye was physically blind, it would allow me to see other worlds more clearly.* I got a little thrill thinking that, but then thought that I could probably do both, as I often had—see other worlds and see the physical world out of that eye, and that's what I wanted.

Jack opened the front door of the truck Ian and I sat in. He grabbed the radio handset. The helo* was on its way and couldn't find us. Unable to get direct comms, the men were having to talk to base, base relaying to the helo. That's how things get screwed up. If the helo couldn't find us, we'd drive to base. I didn't want to have to drive to base. I didn't want fifteen minutes on the road to think about how bad my eye could be, to anticipate getting through the stupid gates. I wanted someone to take charge of my body and move move move. I wanted the medevac helo.

I told myself to quit whining. If we had to drive, that would be interesting in some way, too.

We heard the helo pass over us.

'You just flew over!' Jack shouted into the radio. 'They just passed us!'

'Don't shout,' a calm female voice replied. 'Try to stay calm.'

'I'm not shouting!' Jack yelled.

I grinned—too classic!

'Turn the helo around!' He shouted more softly into the mic. 'We'll pop smoke! Tell him to follow the road back and watch for us—we're deployed' ... something like that. He told them what side of the road, what color smoke—maybe. Something.

Jack got direct comms with the helo about then, according to my possibly faulty memory. I think I remember hearing the pilot's voice on the radio. Things started moving. Jack jumped back out of the truck, and I could see men running and dust clouds billowing outside the window. Within a few minutes, the door beside me opened, and two men helped me out of the truck, pulling my arms over their shoulders.

I might have shouted. My right wrist became a sharp mass of pain as the man on my right pulled it across his shoulder. It didn't slow us down. They ran me to the helo where a medic reached out to help me aboard.

'How are you doing?' he asked me.

I smiled. 'I've had better days,' I admitted. I think he grinned.

I was laid on a stretcher on the helo. Someone ran a blade up my left pant leg, the bloodier one, slicing it cleanly. But maybe that was earlier ... a couple of vignettes have become wanderers in my memory, today happening here, yesterday placing themselves there. The cutting of my trousers is a nomadic event.

100

**I like riding in helos and was curious to see what the inside of the medevac helo looked like. They shot me up with so much morphine, though, I don't remember what it looked like. Darn it.**

My injuries included broken teeth (some of which took a quick exit through my face), a heel broken by shrapnel; small shrapnel scattered in one leg, a broken wrist, a shattered forearm (ulna *and* radius), right hand littered with shrapnel, a hole in my skull exposing the frontal sinus, a skull fracture (isn't that redundant?), shrapnel in both eyes and in my face and sinus, blunt force trauma injuries to one eye (which eventually led to a retinal detachment), and all the bones on the right side of my face broken.

One distraught medic told a friend that my hands were such a mess that my right hand might be useless and that in any case I might not pull through at all with the hole in my head. (This has been the best injury for jokes—think about it.)

As I admitted to the helo medic, I'd had better days!

The most effortless application of expanded awareness is the unconscious one. Our culture teaches us that intuition is *just* imagination, coincidence is random fluke, and flashes of inspiration are the subconscious inexplicably making some new connections. Call it instinct, hunch, intuition, or subconscious direction, I know these moments as communication: the Whole Self has found a clear path through a busy and belief-littered conscious mind. Expanded consciousness continuously communicates with the conscious mind's perception. How could it be otherwise? I am both focused and expanded consciousness. I am one personality.

After reading the first eight chapters, specific examples of expanded awareness at work within my post-blast account might be obvious. I knew immediately, for instance, before I even opened my eyes, that we'd been hit with an IED* and that the results were more than just a few scratches all around (a result more common than one might imagine). I knew that it had been Mark who had died, though it could just as well have been Ben, missing inches of his femoral artery. I also knew that I would live and recover—not that I would necessarily be in the same shape as I'd been prior to the incident, but I would be a workable version of my former self. It never even crossed my mind that my hand wouldn't work or that I would die from the head injuries.

Rather than picking apart these and other specific aspects of my experience and possibly insulting the reader's own ability to connect the details to ideas already presented in this book, I prefer to focus on a portion of the incident that encompasses what I find to be one of the most intriguing aspects of expanded awareness: the mystery of why I was unable to see anyone except the men who interacted directly with me. Over twenty armed men were on the scene. They were guarding the perimeter and moving around within the perimeter working on Ben, Mark, and Ian. I was later told that a good number of Iraqis stopped their cars and gathered at our perimeter to see what was going on. One man tried to cross the perimeter, causing some tense moments for our guards and colleagues. Yet while I periodically looked around trying to see what everyone was up to, I saw *no one at all* unless they interacted directly with me in some way.

When I view the incident from expanded awareness, it's like watching multiple scenes interwoven and overlaid upon each other. All the people in the scene are actively exploring their own probable realities, merging at times with other peoples' chosen paths, then moving back out into their own separate experiences, combining with a small group or nearly the whole group, then splitting back off. Instantaneous decisions are made by our *Whole Selves*; instantaneous combinations and cooperative agreements are formed, discarded, and re-formed in another combination. The whole scene is extremely fluid and complex, yet it moves smoothly and with an oddly fine harmony. As physical time progresses, agreements begin to coalesce, gathering more people into choreographed interaction until the moment when the helo arrives, and everyone's actions join in a symphony of collective focus. At this junction of time, everyone's actions interact directly with each other's, in a sense solidifying one version of collective experience.

This is a difficult concept, being so weirdly foreign to the standard beliefs that structure our perception. An illustration might assist in understanding what I perceive to be happening. Perhaps the reader recalls a classic English creative writing class assignment wherein students are asked to choose a short article from the newspaper and turn it into a full fictional account, creating the back-story of the article. The student makes up the circumstances, sets the scene, creates three-dimensional personalities for the characters, and describes the action leading up to the short incident reported in the newspaper article. For our purposes, imagine that twenty students were given the following news article:

**Two US Army civilians and one security contractor were severely injured in a roadside bomb attack in southern Iraq today. Another security contractor was killed in the attack. The vehicle in which the four were traveling was one of a four-vehicle personal security convoy escorted by Iraqi Police. The injured personnel were air-evacuated to [xx] Air Base near the city of [xx], where they were stabilized before being flown to Balad, Iraq for further stabilization and emergency surgery prior to being evacuated to Germany.**

For this illustration, let's assume the twenty writing students had all worked in southern Iraq for at least six months, either as civilian government employees or as personal security

103

contractors. This will assume that each creative writer shares with the others at least some rudimentary information about the environment and setting, personal security companies and vehicles, the standard response of a team to an emergency situation, and various other useful details. Even with that shared base, there will likely be wildly varied versions of the action among the twenty stories, along with some surprising similarities and overlaps.

Now imagine that each different story written by these creative students was being acted out, all on one stage and at the same time. Each of the twenty stories would have a full complement of actors; let's say thirty people. Aside from the four principals, there would be two Army civilians, one US Army Reserve sergeant, one US Navy Reserve commander, ten personal security guards, and twelve Iraqi Police. Twenty stories multiplied by thirty personnel makes three hundred figures on stage. To approximate the ease with which I perceive the action to have occurred in the real incident, it might help to imagine the actors on stage as ghosts. The ghosts are ephemeral enough to move through solid objects, including each other.

All of the twenty creative stories would include the two scenes in the original article: the moment of the blast and the air evac. Between those two collectively agreed upon actions, the twenty stories will differ. Yet within some of the stories written by the twenty students, certain actions might show up in three of the stories, or eight, or sixteen. The only time one writer's ghosts will interact with another's is when the two (or six, or seventeen) stories include a nearly identical action within the scene. Otherwise, the actors move through each other, each group acting out its own scene without interference. For instance, let's say four stories nearly identically describe the blown up truck rolling down the road, turning off onto the desert. Imagine that sixteen of the stories nearly identically describe the other team vehicles converging around the blown up truck, and seven stories describe the team leader opening one of the doors on the blown up truck. Assume that two stories are nearly identical in their description of men administering First Aid to one of the victims, and two others are identical in their description of men helping another victim out of the blown up vehicle and into another vehicle.

You the reader can continue imagining your own examples of moments or details that are shared by some of the stories and the many ways in which the stories never overlap each other. I'm not big on math, but I suspect someone could break the twenty stories down into units of action for each of the three hundred ghosts on stage, then cross reference those units among all twenty stories and three hundred ghosts and come up with an astronomical number of possible points of overlap and difference.

Within the ghosts' complex matrix of overlapping action, time and space must be understood as Time/Space, so that although a nearly identical action takes place at an estimated ten minutes after the blast in one story and fourteen minutes after the blast in another story, assume that the ghosts acting out the action will intersect at that junction of action as if no time difference existed. And I apologize for this, but to complicate matters further, keep in mind that one story may attribute an action to men A, B, and C while another story attributes the same action to B, D, and Z.

All the actions that are shared between stories will look like convergence points on the stage full of ghosts with action suddenly coalescing in this corner of the stage while flowing back apart and coming together on another area of the stage.

Obviously from a physical consciousness perspective, this would all look impossibly chaotic and aggravatingly incomprehensible. Yet there is sense to each action within each story. There is order in every scene. And as the air evac moment nears, all these impossibly complex, overlapping and separate strings of action begin to merge on the evacuation, coalescing into that more-or-less collective interaction.

In fact, even the details of the collective action of evacuation will differ—an example of the *continuous* exploration of probable realities that I suspect we experience as Whole Beings while we focus within physical reality.

This is the closest illustrative description that I can give of what I perceive to be the reality behind my inability to see any action at the scene in the aftermath of the blast. In talking with the others involved in the incident, we find that our memories don't match up in time sequence or in details of action. As one small example, Ben is convinced that the window beside him was blown out entirely while I vividly remember seeing the Iraqi policeman look in at us through the gun port, which was still in place, set into the glass of Ben's window. Perhaps we're both correct.

My understanding is that the exploration of probable realities is a constantly occurring activity for all of us. Optional realities and paths of experience are perpetually created, formed, and chosen or discarded as a path of focus. Yet we've taught ourselves to sublimate this complexity. We tune out the creative back-story of fluid probable realities. We teach children how to order perception in a way that we've been taught, creating and maintaining a specific version of our functioning world, focusing on some things, and relegating others to *imagination* for reasons that we've lost track of but that must have once served—and still serve—our Whole Selves' creative purpose. The tight focus we've chosen to highlight doesn't negate the fact that this creative exploration goes on all the time; it only blinds us to the process.

In this context, I wasn't seeing individuals moving around the scene of the incident unless they interacted directly with me because I occupied a unique string of reality, only occasionally drifting into a junction with the others. One thought that I had while lying on the ground admiring the blue sky was that in the silence, it felt as if I was in *between* everything that must be happening around me. Perhaps I was.

As one might imagine, this aspect of the experience has provided me with hours of imaginative entertainment. My ideas about time, space, and reality continue to be transformed by this concept the longer I carry it around. It can make my head spin, to tell the truth. If my understanding of this portion of my experience is correct, my personal history becomes a much more complex picture. When I remember something from my childhood that no one else in the family remembers, for instance, perhaps this phenomenon explains it: perhaps we split off into different probable realities and rejoined after experiencing different events. Taking it a step further, combining probable realities with simultaneous Time/Space suggests that the past itself (as well as the future) can actually be altered through intent, through thought, at any point that we take the time to re-imagine the scene.

I sometimes wonder what others who run across these concepts of Time/Space and probable realities (psychics, mystics, cutting edge quantum physicists, people we call mentally ill) think about as they drive home from work, or as they argue with the car repair shop, or as they watch the nightly news. I wonder how they handle what others consider rote interactions with other people or how they think about daily decisions and choices.

How do they respond, for example, when someone says something so simple as "Well, we only have one life to live!" Do they laugh and say (dork alert!), "Actually, we may live an infinity of lives all within a moment—or outside of time if you prefer, and by infinity I mean it—*infinity*! Every choice, every decision you've ever thought about for even an instant has been created and follows its own path and may actually cross and join back up with your own. Or not!"

Of course, they or I don't say that, but that sort of thing will run through my mind. Sometimes I tie myself in mental knots trying to figure out what a culturally appropriate response might be to a companion's casual remark, especially if I've been drifting off on my own, exploring an application of expanded awareness to some stray situation that has popped into my mind: laundry, war in Afghanistan, a mosquito bite, the politics of South Africa, siblings, tsunamis, or volcanoes . . . Something as innocuous as a stranger asking where I'm from can toss me into whirlpools of confusion. Collective reality can seem as completely alien and bizarre to me as the paranormal—or quantum physics—must seem to most people.

This world as we know it through daily life, the media, shared experiences, cultural rules and mores, religious doctrine, political power, all our tiny and broad beliefs—this is the collective cooperative reality *for the moment*. In order to interact without being tossed into a mental institution, it's often necessary to negotiate with myself, choosing when and where it's appropriate to focus down to the pinpoint of physical life as it is and when it might serve to expand my awareness. Intriguing as all this conceptual perception-shifting is, grounding myself in physical life, in the practical, in the version of reality that's collectively agreed upon at the present time, *is* important to me. I chose a physical life in this focus and this time-frame, so it seems logical to participate.

In fact, a friend recently asked what I consider to be the most practically useful knowledge gained through this entire experience of being blown up and having an OBE. Among all the potentially mind-blowing (bad pun intended) and perception-altering concepts that I've encountered, what I most value is that which is applicable daily within the physical focus of what we collectively agree to call our world.

The most broadly practical and useful way in which expanded awareness has influenced my experience has to do with emotions. Although the quiet mayhem described in my version of the incident and its resulting aftermath may sound like a traumatic experience, I've never felt traumatized by it or by the following months of stitches, drugs, needles, surgeries, x-rays, therapies, or even bureaucracy (it's really best to be a soldier, not a civilian GS-government service-employee, if you're going to be treated in a military hospital!). I recall moments of disappointment that I'd created and agreed to maintain a strange and inconvenient effect on vision and some hours of worry and effort, resisting the worst case scenario, when the state of my eye was still unknown, and then again when it was known and weirder than I'd have liked (a variation on double vision). I had a few days (okay, weeks ... well, yes, months) of excruciating pain in my arm that I would have traded off quite cheerfully. Yet a sense of suffering was and is entirely absent from the experience.

From the physical world perspective, getting *excited* about the possibility of being blind in one eye is certainly a novel and possibly mentally deranged way to think about what could be a very inconvenient loss. Yet sitting in the scorched Land Cruiser, that's honestly what I felt: excited about the prospect in a moment of pure joy untainted by how I *should* feel and devoid of fear. This would not have been my normal way of thinking prior to being blown up. Although I've always reacted to emergency situations with unusual calm, "glass half full" wasn't really my thing. This was a physical world moment informed by a clear shot of expanded awareness and its eager curiosity for the possibilities in *any* experience. Remembering the lucid dream with my grandmother was the trigger, a reminder of the playful beauty of new things. "You don't need eyes to see" was also a reminder of what is real. What is enduring and real is the Whole Self, which is not dependent upon the physical body for sight—or hearing, feeling, taste, or scent. Nor is it dependent upon the ability to think logically, do math, fit into a cultural norm, write a complete sentence, or any other perceived necessity. With or without any one or more of our valued senses or abilities, we are still whole, complete personalities living full and meaningful lives within a physical focus.

Lying in the hospital after my retina had been tacked back on and the implications of that surgery described to me, I couldn't find that same thrill in contemplating a one-eyed existence. Yet I felt an amused indifference. *If I can only see out of one eye,* I thought, *It doesn't matter. It's not for that long.*

*Not for that long!* It could be another fifty years!

That thought seems at least as seriously deranged as having felt excited about losing sight in one eye. The thought certainly surprised me as soon as it popped into my head. I'm a visual artist, primarily a visual person, and would have predicted that if I lost sight in one eye I'd be half panicked, angry, depressed. In fact, later I'd be momentarily unable to find this connection to expanded awareness and would cry when talking to my retinal surgeon about the possibility that I wouldn't be able to see out of that eye. *I'm an artist—I really want both eyes!*

How do I describe the strange double awareness that seemed to unfold inside me while I was crying? I was fully engaged in the frustration and fear at the same time that a deeper part of me was *observing* my participation in the physical and amused by my choosing to believe in that perspective.

These moments are now always accessible to me, immediately arresting occasional freefalls into frustration or fear. "It's not that long. This is different—it could be fun." Four months, four years, forty or fifty years … it's just a blink. I'd never been blown up before, and I find an obscene number of things to laugh about within it. In the aftermath, with a sort of double vision and touchy right wrist, everything that I used to do without thought is new, and I choose to find that

110

interesting. A wonder and curiosity about the nature of my experience within physical reality—as *I* create and maintain it—is an immovable foundation to even the most ridiculous and dire moments. A sense of humor is appropriate to every situation.

Buddhists have said, "Pain is inevitable; suffering is optional." Understanding that I designed my experience from start to finish and being assured through my experiences out-of-body that my life *as it is* has meaning and value, suffering is impossible. Even coming to consciousness in a charred truck sprayed with blood, or lying in a hospital bed curled up in a fetal position in excruciating pain, or puking my guts out from an anesthesia hangover (the worst!), or contemplating fifty years of double vision, I've been reminded of the underlying *joy of being* that I experienced most vividly out-of-body. This is not happiness, which seems to me to be more a response to environment and circumstance than a constant interior state. I can be depressed, fearful, worried, irritated, angry—in other words, unhappy, with my circumstances or environment *while* feeling interested, curious, and even excited about the circumstances or environment, my own creation of it, and my own actions and emotions within it. I don't always enjoy the fact that I'm in *this world*, or enjoy being in *this* particular circumstance, but I always feel the foundational joy of being a conscious, creative, expansive personality exploring experience, and enjoy the humor inherent in that.

Physical existence is unique in offering an amazing array of sensory and emotional experience that is made wildly more intense by being in such clear focus within a physical body. Yet we curtail the passion and vibrancy of that experience in many ways and teach ourselves out of believing that our lives have meaning and value. We're taught that only *these* emotions are healthy or appropriate while those others are signs of flaws. Only *these* personalities are healthy and functional while those others need fixing. Only *these* things are of value (money, objects, acts) while those other things are for the less worthy and less valuable beings. Only *these* things (individuals, objects, or acts) are meaningful while overall life is random and meaningless. Religion insists we're born flawed and must remain ever vigilant to save ourselves. Science seems to imply that we're random beings without value beyond that which we can wrest from the indifferent world in the course of our short and brutish lives. Nature is something to fight and control—it will dispassionately destroy us if we don't pay attention. But my experience insists that these assumptions are incorrect.

In trying to curtail, control, and circumscribe the wide array of creativity available, we steal from ourselves. Making everyone comply with an idea of perfection (personally, politically, religiously, or socially) we admit our own fear of ourselves, a distrust that isn't true. We are not, at heart, evil and flawed. If we expressed only curiosity and admiration for each other's different creative lives instead of trying to fix or save those who are different from us, we might find ourselves in a fascinating world. If we understood that we are deliberate co-creators of the world and all experience within it, relatives of and co-creators with the rocks and grass, trees and tigers, wind and storms and tsunamis, the world might be a very different place. If we understood that we each contribute to the creation of so-called disasters and wars, we might quit creating a "war on this" and a "war on that" and instead imagine a cooperative world, the first step to its creation. We might each find profound meaning in what we now think of as small and insignificant lives, thereby letting go of the desire to impose ourselves on others; we might dispose of the need to impose meaning and value in our lives through the deviance of misapplied competition and violence, instead finding it through harmony.

We're each deliberate beings with detailed cooperative plans for our lives. All free emotions that grow within an awareness of the Whole Self are healthy and appropriate, and

112

all personalities are perfect in their unique expression. If we do nothing but enjoy a day, no matter how small and petty it may seem, we've accomplished something valuable. Everything we do, everything we imagine has value and purpose. Every existence has meaning.

Visiting expanded environments didn't solve all my problems or make me a saint. I still get irritated, angry, disgusted, cranky, melancholy, heartbroken, and fearful. I'm sometimes lazy, scatter-brained, mouthy and impatient. But within or beneath how I feel or how I act, I'm also content in an awareness of the goodness and value of my enduring Whole Self. Every experience contains the potential for joy.

This joy is a universal, I think. A prime number in the equation of life. I don't think that my experiences out-of-body imply that these environments are places that others do or will visit should they have an out-of-body experience. After all, the possibilities of environments are literally infinite, and each of us is unique. We may choose collectively created and maintained environments, or, like beautiful dreams, we may each create transition environments that are private and perfect for ourselves.

What I suspect is universal in the out-of-body experience is discovering and knowing the Self as an enduring being, remembering the overwhelmingly complete reality of joy and love that exists, and the intimate connection each consciousness has with every other consciousness, with creation—All That Is.

Love and joy: those words really are completely inadequate to the experience. In order to be accurate, the words must be understood to be bottomlessly deep and thrillingly effortless, both heavy and feather-light, infinitely complex and stunningly simple. They must be understood to be all-inclusive, not defined within belief systems of good and bad, divine and evil, kind and mean, polite and rude. Joy and love from expanded awareness allows for every being and every experience, affirming that every creation is good and beautiful because we are perpetually and effortlessly and infinitely *good*.

I believe people have the capacity to figure out how to live together even if we disagree, to share even when resources are scarce, and to handle our own fears without taking them out on one another. If we each acted from that understanding of who we really are, what would the world be like?

I used to believe that one person's efforts were too small to make a difference in anything large like war or racism or poverty. Now I'm convinced that each and every consciousness makes a valuable contribution to the world and beyond, no matter how insignificant that person might seem from within our belief structures.

One person changes the world just by *imagining* a more harmonious one. Let's try it.

Natalie in Iraq on "hit" day.

On January 7, 2008 Natalie Sudman and Jarrod Bonnick received the Defense of Freedom Medal at the U.S. Army Corps of Engineers Headquarters in Washington, DC. Both were injured in Iraq on November 24, 2007 when their vehicle struck an improvised explosive device. They were traveling in a convoy to visit water treatment plants in the USACE Gulf Region South District.

The DOD created the Defense of Freedom Medal after September 11, 2001, to honor civilians injured during the attack on the Pentagon. The medal is equivalent to the military Purple Heart and is now awarded to any DOD civilian injured by enemy action in the global war on terrorism.

Sudman, an archeologist with the Bureau of Land Management, had been in Iraq with the USACE since August 7, 2006. She had volunteered to work for the USACE on the Gulf Coast after Hurricane Katrina, and later her USACE friends invited her to work in Iraq. She worked as a project engineer in the Basrah South Regional Office managing a number of projects including a primary health care center at Khor Az Aubair.

Bonnick was a regulatory project manager with the Louisville District and worked with Sudman as a project manager on electricity and water projects in Tallil. He arrived in Iraq on October 20. The day of the attack was his first trip to project sites and only his second time off the base in Tallil. Both sustained serious injuries in the explosion.

** Taken from Army AL&T Online Web-exclusive Articles, by Bernard Tate.    June 2008
**USACE photo by F.T. Eyre

Back Jacket photo:  President George W. Bush visiting Natalie Sudman in the hospital.

# Glossary

**BDU:** Army battle dress uniform, the brown camouflage pattern also called cammies. We civilians were required to wear our Army uniforms whenever we traveled off base. Most of us felt that wearing these uniforms was like painting a big fat target on our chests—and on the chests of the Iraqis that we met with out in the field. Of course the Army didn't care what we thought.

**Cammies:** camouflage Army uniform, also known as BDU's.

**Comms:** communications

**Digital Cammies:** Battle uniforms with digital fabric pattern

**Helo:** helicopter

**IED:** improvised explosive device. Also commonly called a roadside bomb. Technically we were hit with an EFP, an explosive force penetrator, which is an armor-piercing version of an IED.

**IP:** Iraqi Police. Because governance of the province that I worked in had been formally handed over to the Iraqis, we were required to have an Iraqi Police escort whenever we traveled off base. The skill and professionalism of these police units was uneven and unreliable, and the IP were generally known to be heavily infiltrated with insurgents.

**Long gun:** rifle

**Med kit:** medical kit. Each PSD team convoy had a designated medic on the team, and carried at least one trauma medical kit.

**PSD:** personal security detail. These were contracted security teams who guarded us whenever we traveled off base. Normally we traveled in three vehicle convoys: a lead truck, the "principal" vehicle (those of us being guarded were referred to as "principals"), and the gun truck. Four vehicle convoys like the one we used on the day we were hit with the IED weren't the norm, but weren't uncommon either.

**Running on closed mic:** When running on "closed mic"— closed microphone—all communications between the personal security men in the various trucks took place through headphones or earbuds. The "principals," we the people that they were protecting, were unable to listen in on their observations and conversations. Some of my teams would run on "open mic," which made for a much more informed, interesting, and often amusing ride.

**Natalie Sudman** worked as an archeologist in the Great Basin states for sixteen years before accepting a position managing construction contracts in Iraq. After being injured by a roadside bomb, Natalie retired from government service. She is now enjoying art, writing, and continuing explorations into the non-physical.

Natalie reads and heals psychically, communicates with those who have passed over, and channels non-physical beings. She offers information regarding personal questions as well as addressing broader subjects such as the nature of space, time or reality.

Natalie has a particular interest in the intersections of science and the non-physical. She has been a subject of studies performed by the University of Virginia's Division of Perceptual Studies, and welcomes invitations to act as a lab rat for any scientific investigation. Describing herself as an open-minded skeptic, Natalie finds that the rigorous methodology of science appeals to her critical mind, while her artistic nature enjoys the expansive freedom of leaving behind the critical mind in frequent forays into the non-physical. She maintains that an irreverent sense of humor and a willingness to look foolish are the cornerstones of constructive exploration.

Raised in Minnesota, Natalie has lived most of her adult life in eastern Oregon, Montana and South Dakota. She recently moved to southern Arizona. Her artwork is available through Davis & Cline Galleries in Ashland Oregon, and her urns will be available online in early 2012 at
www.inyantraceartstudio.com

She occasionally blogs at
www.traceofelements.wordpress.com

## Other Books Published by Ozark Mountain Publishing, Inc.

Conversations with Nostradamus, Volume I, II, III...............by Dolores Cannon
Jesus and the Essenes...........................................................by Dolores Cannon
They Walked with Jesus........................................................by Dolores Cannon
Between Death and Life........................................................ by Dolores Cannon
A Soul Remembers Hiroshima..............................................by Dolores Cannon
Keepers of the Garden.........................................................by Dolores Cannon
The Legend of Starcrash.......................................................by Dolores Cannon
The Custodians....................................................................by Dolores Cannon
The Convoluted Universe - Book One, Two, Three, Four......by Dolores Cannon
Five Lives Remembered ......................................................by Dolores Cannon
The Three Waves of Volunteers and the New Earth ............. by Dolores Cannon
I Have Lived Before............................................................by Sture Lönnerstrand
The Forgotten Woman...............................................by Arun & Sunanda Gandhi
Luck Doesn't Happen by Chance...................................by Claire Doyle Beland
Mankind - Child of the Stars............................by Max H. Flindt & Otto Binder
Past Life Memories As A Confederate Soldier.........................by James H. Kent
Holiday in Heaven...............................................................by Aron Abrahamsen
Out of the Archives ....................................... by Aron & Doris Abrahamsen
Is Jehovah An E.T.?..................................................................by Dorothy Leon
The Essenes - Children of the Light..............by Stuart Wilson & Joanna Prentis
Power of the Magdalene...............................by Stuart Wilson & Joanna Prentis
Beyond Limitations .....................................by Stuart Wilson & Joanna Prentis
Atlantis and the New Consciousness ........... by Stuart Wilson & Joanna Prentis
Rebirth of the Oracle.................................by Justine Alessi & M. E. McMillan
Reincarnation: The View from Eternity......by O.T. Bonnett, M.D. & Greg Satre
The Divinity Factor.............................................................by Donald L. Hicks
What I Learned After Medical School ............................by O.T. Bonnett, M.D.
Why Healing Happens........................................................by O.T. Bonnett, M.D.
A Journey Into Being.....................................................by Christine Ramos, RN
Discover The Universe Within You........................................by Mary Letorney
Worlds Beyond Death....................................................by Rev. Grant H. Pealer
A Funny Thing Happened on the Way to Heaven ......... by Rev. Grant H. Pealer
Let's Get Natural With Herbs.................................................by Debra Rayburn
The Enchanted Garden.................................................................by Jodi Felice
My Teachers Wear Fur Coats........................by Susan Mack & Natalia Krawetz
Seeing True.........................................................................by Ronald Chapman
Elder Gods of Antiquity..........................................................by M. Don Schorn
Legacy of the Elder Gods.......................................................by M. Don Schorn
Gardens of the Elder Gods .................................................... by M. Don Schorn
Reincarnation...Stepping Stones of Life ................................by M. Don Schorn

**Continue for more books by Ozark Mountain Publishing, Inc.**

Children of the Stars .............................................................. by Nikki Pattillo
A Spiritual Evolution ............................................................. by Nikki Pattillo
Angels - The Guardians of Your Destiny .............by Maiya & Geoff Gray-Cobb
Seeds of the Soul.................................................by Maiya Gray-Cobb
The Despiritualized Church..........................................by Rev. Keith Bender
The Science of Knowledge ...........................................by Vara Humphreys
The Other Side of Suicide .....................................by Karen Peebles
Journey Through Fear ..........................................by Antoinette Lee Howard
Awakening To Your Creation ...............................................by Julia Hanson
Thirty Miracles in Thirty Days ...................................by Irene Lucas
Windows of Opportunity ...................................................by Sherri Cortland
Raising Our Vibrations for the New Age ........................ by Sherri Cortland
Why? ...........................................................................by Mandeep Khera
The Healing Christ .........................................Robert Winterhalter
Morning Coffee with God ....................................Michael Dennis
God's Many Mansions .................................... by Michael Dennis
Ask Your Inner Voice .........................................by James Wawro
Live From the Other Side .........................by Maureen McGill & Nola Davis
TWIDDERS ...............................................................by Anita Holmes
Evolution of the Spirit.......................................... by Walter Pullen
You Were Destined To Be Together ................................... by Tom Arbino
Teen Oracle .................................................................. by Cinnamon Crow
Chakra Zodiac Healing Oracle ...................................... by Cinnamon Crow
The History of God ........................................................... by Guy Needler
Lifting the Veil on the Lost Continent of Mu ............... by Jack Churchward
The Big E - Everything is Energy ............. by Jarrad Hewett & Dee Wallace
Conscious Creation ............................................................ by Dee Wallace

For more information about any of the above titles, soon to be released titles, or other items in our catalog, write or visit our website:

OZARK
MOUNTAIN
PUBLISHING

PO Box 754
Huntsville, AR 72740
www.ozarkmt.com
1-800-935-0045/479-738-2348
Wholesale Inquiries Welcome